BEAUTIFUL PEOPLE

BEAUTIFUL PEOPLE

WOMEN OF COLOR
DECENTRALIZING INNOVATION IN BEAUTY

SADICHCHHA ADHIKARI

NEW DEGREE PRESS

BEAUTIFUL PEOPLE

WOMEN OF COLOR DECENTRALIZING INNOVATION IN BEAUTY

ISBN   978-1-63730-433-4 *Paperback*

978-1-63730-523-2 *Kindle Ebook*

978-1-63730-524-9 *Ebook*

To all my beautiful people,
you know who you are.

I walk into CVS and go straight to the makeup aisle. I know exactly what I'm looking for. I've searched online for "brown girl makeup," "brown girl foundation," and "dark skin mattifying foundation." I know the brand I need to go for, and I've narrowed it down to two to three shades I should try.

I brought my own makeup sponge with me so I could "sample" from CVS (sorry!). I dab shade A onto my hand then apply to my chin and look at my face in the light, just like the Sephora employees taught me to do. It's a little light. Shade B is a little dark. Shade C, too dark.

I experiment with the products while hiding from the store clerks. My hand looks like a splotchy tapestry of different shades of dark beige, but none that fit me well. I've gotten streaks of foundation on my clothes and have now suspiciously been in the same CVS aisle for twenty-five minutes. Nothing is really blending into my skin. I don't have enough options, but if I come home empty-handed, I'll have to start my research all over again.

Now I'm trying to mix the colors on the back of my hand to see if a mixture works. The generously fluorescent lighting makes things okay. I note the proportions of my concoction and buy Shades A and B.

I go home and give it a try; it doesn't work. I return B and keep Shade A; it doesn't work. I buy Shades B and C and mix them; it doesn't work.

I'm just trying to buy makeup. Not only are drugstore options limited, but I've had so many experiences like this in which 1) there are not a lot of shades catering to my skin tone, and 2) when I do find products, there aren't enough shades to match my skin tone exactly.

Does this happen to everyone? Has this happened to you? Why is it so hard to find makeup?

CONTENTS

———

INTRODUCTION

Once dormant and repetitive, the beauty industry has become explosive and volatile, especially over the past thirty or so years. A *Business Insider* article showed that the global beauty industry is valued at over $530 *billion* and will grow to $716 billion by 2025. This is a shockingly high number. By comparison, US Apparel Market statistics show that the apparel industry is worth $1.9 trillion, which means that even at today's pace, the beauty industry makes up about a quarter of the fashion industry. In other words, one industry in which consumerism is primarily driven by a far smaller population of those who identify as women can be financially compared to the clothing industry, with a much larger consumer base.

The origins of this industry are deeply rooted in western beauty ideals. The very few scholars, sociologists, anthropologists, and others who have studied beauty ideals have often noted the industry's association with whiteness. One example is commonly seen when considering this connection—how western beauty ideals have manifested in and been perpetuated by Miss America pageants. In fact, Leah Donella writes in *NPR*'s Code Switch that not until 1940 were women of color allowed to enter the Miss America pageant. So until 1940, the imagery associated with American beauty was limited to a "thin, blonde, blue-eyed white woman."

This is just one of many examples. Unfortunately, there are more instances like this. Consider products designed to make your skin whiter (looking at you, Fair & Lovely), or the South Korean plastic surgery market, for another example. Or, most familiar to us all, just look at most of the celebrities and influencers we see succeeding on TV screens, magazines, and everywhere else. Most of these examples tend to get consumers closer to fitting these white beauty ideals.

What does this historical landscape of beauty ideals mean for today's consumers? In other words, how are products being developed for and targeted toward women today? Putting it very generally, if you are an American cosmetics company and you have been successfully profiting for decades by creating products primarily for people to fit this beauty ideal (aka white women), why would you change your ways? Why would you choose to stop benefiting from a $530 billion industry?

"The bottom line is always to sell products," according to Phyllis Ellis, creator of the documentary *Toxic Beauty*. If this is the case, then product development becomes a self-fulfilling prophecy of products doing well because they are primarily created and marketed to white women. Certain products don't do well because, for example, people like me can't find a good concealer shade to match our skin, so the return for the cosmetics company is lower and so, then, is the investment in these products. It's a vicious cycle of less diverse products doing poorly on the market because the items developed for a diverse consumer base tend not to work well. It's not a problem of supply and demand—there is absolutely demand from women of color for good makeup; it's that the supply is simply not there.

As a result of this cycle, the development of products that are suitable for women of "nontraditional" shades are lower, thereby decreasing availability of these products, thereby decreasing revenue from these products, thereby decreasing investment in these products, thereby decreasing the development of these products, and on and on.

Unfortunately for the beauty industry, product development is led primarily by seven conglomerates that are making most of the go-to-market decisions. For a homogeneous industry like this, I argue that it takes women, like the women in this book, to innovate the industry by bringing diversity in the products they create in order to truly cause disruption and change. Although the examples I've highlighted thus far are focused on the lack of shade ranges for skin cosmetics, we'll see later in this book examples of women who have created all kinds of inclusive beauty products that go beyond foundation and concealer.

Vicky Tsai started Tatcha because, during a trip to Japan, she found inspiration and differentiation in the products geisha had been using for over three hundred years. Huda Kattan started Huda Beauty because she wasn't able to find products to help enhance her Middle Eastern features. Nancy Twine started Briogeo because she could not find natural hair care products that would perform as promised on her hair.

These are just three out of eight stories highlighted in the book, and these stories are eight out of hundreds of women of color tapping into their heritage, their culture, their skin, and their hair, decentralizing and individualizing the beauty industry. We need choices, we need options, we need more representation of different types of women wearing these products, we need these products tested on different women, and we need to make sure these products show up well on us all.

Why do we need options? For one, because there are women of different color and cosmetic needs who deserve to see their needs met on the shelves of CVS and Sephora. More than that, though, not expanding product offerings to be more inclusive reinforces antiquated ideals of beauty and, therefore, delays the progression we are making for beauty products to fit the needs of all women. Unrealistic and unattainable beauty standards, or hyper-Westernized beauty standards in the case of the beauty industry, will also continue to perpetuate colorism and, therefore, discrimination of people who have darker skin.

On the flip side of the coin, the incentive for big cosmetic companies is largely financial. In an industry that has already surpassed $530 billion largely by releasing similar products over and over again, the landscape of products offered has changed so much that inclusion in beauty means a new customer base is ripe for the taking. How ripe? Just one 2019 Nielsen study showed that when it comes to beauty products, Black Americans outspent other groups by 19 percent, amounting to $572.6 million worth of revenue.

I'm a woman of color telling you that I, and other women like me, have trouble finding makeup that fits my skin tone, trouble finding makeup that helps me deal with dark circles, skin texture, hair texture, sun protection, and other issues that come up when products are not made for people like me. There's also the "this eye shadow is too powdery and light to show up on my skin" problem that I have encountered with almost all "nude" shadow palettes.

This isn't to say that white people are responsible for steering the industry in a certain direction. The fact that I have to share this disclaimer shows even my own insecurity in talking about beauty ideals developing from whiteness. I also don't want the assumption of this book to be that I am calling out white people for buying makeup made for white people. Keep doing what you're doing if you've found what works for you. However, I think we can all consider the fact that if there are only really a handful of companies producing inclusive products out of the many brands we know and love, it will be hard to innovate and differentiate without contributing to this system.

If I ask you to think of a brand that has revolutionized inclusivity in makeup, you'll likely think of Rihanna's Fenty Beauty. Despite not being the first company to have a forty-shade range for foundations, being one of the first companies to *market* itself as an inclusive brand, backed by Rihanna's name recognition, made it so that inclusion became table stakes for beauty products. This Fenty movement started in 2017, though. Despite the visibility of Fenty Beauty, there are stories of women who came before Rihanna, who used their backgrounds and experiences in the industry to realize that their needs are the missing piece of the market in the beauty industry and decided to do something about it.

These women, who have really innovated the industry, have disrupted this conglomerate-driven model so much that the industry has now shifted to an independent brand-, personalization-, inclusion-, and strongly consumer-driven model. These women have created successful companies through their innovation and have not only helped introduce some much-needed differentiation in the industry but have also paved the way for new, similar companies to emerge. The more you chip away and break down a large system, the more it creates space for other brands to emerge. It also forces the conglomerates to think about what they can do to stay relevant in a changing industry. These women, in other words, have effectively contributed to decentralizing innovation in an industry worth over $530 billion.

The women I write about are women of color. My intention is not for this book to be focused on the hardships of immigrants or the ladders these women had to climb to fight for the empires they created, although that's a reality for all of them. My intention, instead, is to highlight their success in pushing the envelope of what's considered beautiful.

This book is for anyone who is interested in the beauty industry, understanding the innovative powers of knowing and loving where you come from, and figuring out a way to share it with others. It is also a book for people who want to hear the stories of women who have found success in challenging long-standing ideals, and it's for those of you who want to get a head start on the future of beauty.

The beauty industry is teeming with innovation and the opportunity to create. The velvet ropes that once separated this industry from outsiders are now being shred apart by the transparency that the digital world has thrust upon us. The industry is being challenged by today's consumers, so much so that it will inevitably lead to exciting changes. Things will evolve, more people will share their stories, new products will emerge, and we'll have more choices—why not take part?

PART 1

DIFFERENCES

———

It was a Sunday afternoon, and the sun was barely trickling into my studio apartment that sadly faces the wall of another building. I had a call set up with a beauty executive, who happened to be one of the first white women I was interviewing for this book. I looked forward to it, coffee ready to go, and was excited for her insights as an experienced trend forecaster in the beauty industry.

I got a lot out of that conversation; she was smart and well-versed in the world of beauty business and had an almost uncanny confidence in her vision for the future of beauty. I loved it. I asked her about her background and how she came up in the industry, and as she was describing her career, I noticed something right away. There was a drastic and stark difference between the way she described her path to success in beauty and the same story I heard from a Black executive.

I spoke to a Black executive who began her career in beauty working for a magazine for Black women. Her path to success seemed constantly riddled with hurdles. In trying to move forward with her career, she described that it was "very difficult to find bylines at mainstream outlets," which "could've been because of lack of representation and biases in the stories I was interested in writing, or it could've been that I didn't have access to the necessary networks." More likely than not, it was a combination of both. The historical preference for white-centric beauty ideals, the lack of representation of people of color in the beauty industry, and the many barriers to entry in this space mean that if you had a background in promoting beauty for people of color, you'd likely have a hard time advancing to mainstream work.

Compare this with the conversation I had with the white executive. Although they came from similar backgrounds, her tone was very different. Contrasting with the Black executive, the white executive had a very relaxed way of describing her process of moving up the beauty ladder. She said, "I'm just really curious, or I get bored easily, but there's always a clear moment to me where it's like I've done what I can with this business; it's time for me to turn it over to somebody else." Her career "evolved organically," and she was able to take advantage of her path, which has been like a "staircase, like, one thing that leads you somewhere and then you have a set of choices that will lead you in different directions and then you're kind of building on it." This description sounded so passive to me, especially against the backdrop of my conversation not only with the Black executive above but virtually every other conversation in this book.

I will leave the originators of these stories unnamed because I want it to be clear that this experience is not tied to a specific person. This type of narrative and social divide is applicable for every person of color. Yes, these are just two out of many career stories, but the hardships showcased by my conversation with the Black executive and the casual and opportunistic way in which the white executive describes her career trajectory—completely different ends of the spectrum if you ask me.

HISTORY OF BEAUTY

In doing research for this book, I came across a 1987 *Washington Post* article, "Beauty Through History." The key question this article was asking, "Where is the face that would launch a thousand ships today?" warranted a slew of answers from industry leaders. Okay, I see Bette Midler, a very beautiful white woman. Others mention Linda Evans, Kathleen Turner, then comes Rita Hayworth and Debra Winger—okay. Meryl Streep and Sissy Spacek are described to "have prized the quirky beauty of a modern movie star," then Greta Garbo, Grace Kelly, Ingrid Bergman, Doris Day, and Debbie Reynolds, who all have one thing in common—they are all white women.

Sure, it's *one* article, but this article showcases a much larger case for the way representation works in the beauty industry. The history of beauty, and the way the business itself has developed, is very white-centric. Mainly driven by cultural depictions of beauty in television, the access, availability, and resources that white Americans disproportionately have makes it so that the availability of beauty products, the affiliated marketing, and therefore the ideals of beauty have also become very westernized.

What Scholars Say

First, I should mention that the scholarship on the beauty industry, particularly business cases for understanding changes in this industry, is extremely limited. *Hope in a Jar: The Making of America's Beauty Culture* by Kathy Peiss, published in 1998, is one of the more comprehensive pieces on the history of how the beauty industry became commercialized. Peiss, a professor at the University of Pennsylvania, exposes the drastically evolving nature of how beauty has developed. From a business perspective, the beauty industry has been largely built by women and has allowed women to seize "their chances, becoming entrepreneurs, inventors, manufacturers, distributors, and promoters." Peiss even argues that "many of the most successful entrepreneurs were immigrant, working-class, or black women," who played a central role in the early movements to redefine beauty ideals.

The concept of female entrepreneurs in beauty is not a new phenomenon. Prominent beauty influencers, even women of color (Madam C. J. Walker, for example), are a familiar part of entrepreneurial history. Despite a promising head start for women in the industry, the early 1900s brought "an emergent class of managers and professionals [who] were developing new methods that would come to dominate American business." This emergent class in business was mostly made up of men who were educated and trained for the "national system of mass production, distribution, marketing, and advertising that transformed local patterns of buying and selling and fostered a culture of consumption." Mass production meant a growing demand for products and a disconnect from the beauty salon-oriented, intimate buying behavior of beauty to one focused on mass production and large-scale exchange of products.

Because of this changing industry, "men with little cosmetic expertise saw easy money in selling beauty and hustled into the trade." Of course, women still participated in the industry, but the business acumen needed to stay competitive in this bustling market limited opportunities for growth, causing the entities once owned by women to be passed over to large companies controlled by men.

Despite beauty having a woman-led consumer base, I was still quite surprised to read that women pioneered the development of the business industry. This feeling of surprise likely stems from the fact that today, there is a large discrepancy in female representation in beauty C-suites. Despite the fact that women are more represented in the C-suite spaces today, and despite the fact that the companies addressed in this book are female founded, Allison Collins's "Are Women Moving Up Beauty's Corporate Ladder?" shows that as of 2021, "women hold only 15 percent of CEO titles in the top twenty beauty manufacturers. This is true for many of the reasons women are not well-represented in C-suites overall—business bias and discrimination, systemic issues that don't allow for these opportunities to come up, and so on and so forth.

The beauty industry for the Black community, which Peiss thankfully covers relatively extensively, also followed a similar pattern of development, but progress in this community was even more limited. Because progress was limited, this subset of the industry was partially immune from the dramatic shift that the larger companies created. The beauty business in the Black community did expand with the help of magazines and mass media outlets that specifically addressed Black women, and demand grew accordingly. But alas, much like *literally* everything else, white entrepreneurs experienced in the world of beauty recognized the growing market and demand of products for the Black community. As a result, the same white men who realized the competitive cosmetics market started commoditizing products for Black women as well.

So it is in this way that the history of this industry is not unfamiliar with female entrepreneurship or women of color contributing heavily to the industry. However, inequalities plagued by many societal factors meant that ownership of production, marketing, competition, and all aspects of growing a business kept bouncing around from white women and women of color and eventually fed into the business conglomerate system. The end result of these shifts is beauty as we know it today, an industry driven by a conglomerate model, primarily run by men.

What Other Scholars Say

More recent scholarship in this field does exist, but the business case for beauty is still extremely limited. I went to business school and was only able to delve into this industry a few times when options for projects were primarily student driven. Otherwise, the cases assigned to us, I swear, were always about Trader Joe's or Southwest Airlines. I suspect there are some gender bias issues that have led to this dearth in scholarship, but Harvard Business School professor Geoffrey Jones, in 2010's *Beauty Imagined: A History of the Global Beauty Industry,* has produced one of the more comprehensive pieces describing how the business of beauty has developed in the past one-hundred-plus years.

Jones argues, supplementing Peiss's overarching narrative of how production in this industry has developed, that as we reached modernization in the nineteenth century, it allowed for the beauty industry to begin mass-producing products. This homogenized the industry and created an industry in which "beauty became associated with Western countries, and white people." The role of industrialization in the beauty industry, then, became about reinforcing these ideals. The contribution of this industry became to "turn these underlying trends into brands, create aspirations that drove their growing use, and employ modern marketing methods to globalize them."

It is in this way that this industry became the self-fulfilling prophecy I described in the previous chapter. Consumers develop an ideal for beauty (white-centric), then the industry responds to that ideal and continues to advertise for that ideal until younger views of beauty also follow this ideal, and so the cycle continues. You could ask the question of which one came first, the beauty ideals or the products developed to fulfill these ideals. But for me, the takeaway is that over time, beauty preferences have become systemic and beauty products to match these preferences have largely "whitened" what ideal beauty looks like.

Today, we are seeing the homogeneity in demand of beauty products being driven by homogenous business practices, exemplified by pieces like "These seven companies control almost every single beauty product you buy." More specifically, this homogeneity is driven by L'Oréal, Johnson & Johnson, Shiseido, Estée Lauder, Unilever, P&G, and Coty, who own and operate over 182 beauty brands we all use. These megabrands "are responsible for controlling advertising and the way we all think about beauty every day," and these companies, across the board, are likely using the same manufacturers, formulas, and (male) scientists to develop these products. So what does the industry, product development, innovation, and its impacts on the life of an entrepreneur in this space look like when the operations are being carried out in this way?

Donna

Donna Lopez is the founder and CEO of Making Lemonade, an empowered beauty community that educates and inspires the next generation of beauty bosses. She's been interested in beauty since she was twelve years old and has grown her beauty career from counter to corporate, which is why I was particularly excited to talk to her. She is a really great example of the type of story I want to be telling with this book. Having seen and experienced the entire gamut of what this industry has to offer, and as someone who has helped companies develop products both from the corporate side and now as an owner of her own business, she has a well-versed pulse on the industry.

Her origin story and her fifteen years in the beauty industry highlight three themes that help set the tone for how this industry operates. Donna, having seen this industry from counter to corporate, has a unique ability to share this insight with us.

Access

Donna described the beauty industry as being "very hidden by velvet ropes." As a newcomer, one is likely to get lost because "there's not a lot of information on the beauty industry, there's not a lot of information on how to start a product, there's not really information about anything." If you are not familiar with the inner workings of this industry and you don't have a lot of contacts, it's very hard to be an innovator and an independent product creator in this space.

To be involved in beauty, "you kind of have to either get a job at some big conglomerate, or live in New York, LA, or San Francisco." Those were really your options to develop as a professional in the beauty industry ten to twenty years ago. Even if you were interested in being part of the conglomerate rather than starting your own company, "there is no information about having a career in the beauty industry, there were no classes, no education, no school to go to about how to get into corporate beauty."

Even doing research for this book, I've realized that the professional beauty industry is really hard to enter as an outsider. First of all, it's been hard to find connections to interview without knowing a lot of key players in the industry, but I've found that once you speak to the PR team in one company, you can get easily connected to teams in another company. So again, keeping in mind the way this industry has developed and knowing how the professional relationships in this industry are formed, it's difficult to find an "in." This barrier is likely exacerbated for members of marginalized communities for many reasons—for one, it's expensive to live in New York, LA, or San Francisco. Knowing that it's a difficult industry to enter, would you have the wherewithal to keep searching? Would you have the access and the resources to start your own product line to address this missing piece of the market?

Success in this industry is not a reality for everyone, but it was for the women who are highlighted in this book. We'll see that even for the women profiled in this book, their ventures were supported by a background in business, an internet presence, financial support, strong connections in the beauty industry, or a lucky combination of all four.

Inclusion

Inclusion in products has been an afterthought for product development in this market. Donna once had a conversation with a supervisor who, when asked why they nixed the darker shades from their shelves, responded, "Think about it logically; Black skin doesn't wear a lot of foundation." I was shocked to hear this, but Donna said these conversations were common ten years ago and not a lot of people questioned it. "I was actually told to shut up about it," Donna recalled not so fondly. Companies would discontinue deeper shades without a thought, oftentimes because of their own preconceived notions, and other times, these were decisions made by manufacturers to protect from cannibalization of their own products. In other words, if you are a manufacturer developing the same products for the same companies, you'll want to be selective about the shades you choose to manufacture so as to not take over sales for the shade range offerings of the other brands you support.

Rea Ann Silva of Beautyblender told me about the "lack of diversity within the cosmetic companies within the shade range, just because they wanted to cater to productive colors." The "productive" colors she referenced were more of the beige-white shades that tend to have more options that would fit the skin tone of white women and would therefore sell well. Business decisions to create more shades for white buyers, according to Rea Ann, came from "prejudicial belief systems, about access to cash, the ability to spend on beauty."

Donna also talked about the buyer side of things when it comes to product selection. "Diversity is so important… but the reality is… there's still minimum quantities you have to place with a manufacturer, but there genuinely aren't enough people buying all shades consistently." When you are continuously benefiting from selling certain products (lighter shades), and you're not seeing the same return from other products (darker shades), you're going to invest in research and development for products with a higher return on investment. It goes to show how this industry has developed, that the return on investment is coming from homogeneity in products made for white women.

One company many of my interviewees, and even friends, bring up when I talk about women of color in beauty entrepreneurship is Fenty Beauty. I mentioned this in the last chapter, but Fenty Beauty, founded by Rihanna in 2017, gained a lot of traction mainly for its inclusive product line but also for including diverse faces in the marketing and branding of the company. Rihanna was the first to use her fame and fortune to boast the inclusive foundation shade line, include all types of women in marketing materials, engage influencers of color, and really put inclusion at the core of all her products. In the lipstick and highlighter offerings, for example, they thought about the compatibility of these colors with all types of skin tones, and when I looked at their products online, I was able to find someone with almost exactly my complexion and be able to decide how the product would look on me without having to buy and try.

Again, Fenty Beauty was certainly not the first company to have such a wide range of foundations, but it is the first one to shout it from the rooftops and make it so shade inclusion became a criterion by which customers would judge the diversity factor of your products. Rea Ann Silva of Beauty-blender talked about what Rihanna's brand name has done for the beauty industry and said, "Hats off to her. She's done an amazing job and continues to just evolve and do amazing things. Thank God for her because it took someone like her to really bring this issue to the forefront so that everybody understands it now. It makes it easier for brand founders like myself who really wanted passivity and diversity and the need for complexion shade range."

Digital

In *Beauty Imagined,* Jones also argues that the introduction of new technologies has catalyzed different uses of beauty products in various ways. Some innovations are obvious contributors to expanding beauty products, including the invention of hygiene products like soap and toothpaste. Other inventions are more indirect, like the invention of television, after which people were able to rely on channels like the Home Shopping Network (HSN) and Quality Value Convenience (QVC) to learn about new products and, of course, more recently, the use of social media and influencer marketing to expand brand awareness.

One of Donna's many roles in corporate beauty has been gearing companies up for digitization and e-commerce. With the emergence of channels like HSN and QVC, you have to sell products in three minutes, and you have to meet sales goals by the minute. According to Donna, the viewers of these channels were mostly white women; the biggest return the sellers could get was by solely showing the lighter shades on TV. With the emergence of e-commerce, platforms like

HSN/QVC were finally able to expand their offerings on their websites.

Donna also continued to work with other brands to expand product inclusion in the digital space, eventually working with Instagram and TikTok influencers to pioneer the partnership of the digital and beauty world. Hannah Gnegy in "Beauty and the Brand" describes how YouTube emerged as "one of the first social network platforms to offer revenue for producing videos," and the emergence of Facebook, Instagram, and now TikTok followed suit with similar payment models. In fact, 82 percent of businesses stated that they either fully integrated or were in the process of fully integrating their brands into the digital world.

I sometimes question whether brands are able to sell through social media authentically. Are brands genuinely able to get their message across when working with influencers? On the one hand, the influencers may lie about the efficacy of the products to preserve brand deals, but on the other hand, I would argue, the trust they have built with their audience and the followship that comes with this trust is far more valuable. So, I view this hurdle as a positive return for the customer in that the information consumers are getting is being filtered through (mostly) honest reviews posted by influencers. This means that the development of consumer voices in the digital world has become a lot more apparent.

Market Size

Donna's story also highlights the breadth of opportunity in beauty. The rapid development of this industry is all made possible by the fact that beauty is a very lucrative path. This industry is *wealthy* and is growing at an exponential speed. When Jones wrote his book ten years ago, he cited the global beauty industry as being worth $330 billion. We learned earlier that today, it is worth $530 billion and will grow to $716 billion by 2025. For an industry that is already one of the wealthiest market segments, worth $530 billion, to have grown by 60 percent and then continue to grow by 35% in the future… it's a promisingly lucrative industry to be in.

Because of the "velvet rope" nature of this industry and because it's very connection and relationship driven, access to the secret to financial success in this industry is also limited. I'd imagine with the money available, conglomerates are incentivized to tighten the velvet ropes and make it even more difficult for outsiders to take a cut, creating more difficult barriers to entry.

Donna's story is one of many, but the flow of her work and the experiences she's shared really showcase the fast-growing, rapidly changing, and difficult-to-enter industry that is beauty. The landscape of this business, as we will see in future chapters, is a harsh one. It's not only a difficult industry to get into, but there are a lot of ideals society has built to combat inclusion in this space, *and* everything you do as a founder is immediately available for people to see and potentially criticize.

Despite these major hurdles, we will also see that because of these women, independent brands in makeup have emerged and have become as powerful as they are today. These women have fought through the heavy rubble of this industry to bring their visions to life and have pushed for a dramatic shift that will later help create inspiration, opportunities, and, in some cases, investment avenues for others to follow suit.

PART 2

———

THE PROFILES

———

I've been using some of the products I mention in this book for years. I had no idea the brands I've been using for that long, some for decades, were not just thought up by some product development team in the too-well-lit corner of a sanitized lab. They all have origin stories that are unique. I just always assumed they were all created by some engineering team of one of the conglomerates and not actual humans who have amazing stories to share—until I started doing some digging for the profiles in this book.

The stories of the women I am highlighting showcase examples of the breadth of barriers to entry in the beauty space. Everything from financing, background in beauty, and race and gender can play a detrimental role in one's entry into the beauty space. These stories will help showcase the drastic changes in the beauty industry, and they'll show what women did to get us to this stage of having drastic changes. Breaking up a business system that has been running one way for centuries does not happen overnight. It, in fact, is a system that you slowly chip away at, eventually paving the way for others to join the cause until the conglomerate system is completely dismantled and there is a truly open market for all beauty products to thrive.

At the beginning of this book, I talked about how I wanted to showcase the change in this industry. These women are the drivers of this change. I'll be talking about ten innovators and eight companies in particular, all who realized a gap in the market, all who were inspired and driven by their own experiences to fill these gaps, and all who found success in doing so—ultimately paving the way for others to follow. Following the stories of these super women, we'll be able to see how these founders have changed the system for companies like Rooshy Roy's AAVRANI to emerge.

The companies represented here are ones that are wildly successful and have gained significant name and product recognition. However, these companies don't run the entire gamut of beauty products created by women of color—there are other companies, Divya Gugnani's Wander Beauty, Amy Liu's Tower 28, Cashmere Nicole's Beauty Bakerie, and I'm sure many others that are emerging at a speed at which I can't keep up. There's a whole category of beauty founders from YouTube, Michelle Phan's EM Cosmetics, for example, that I am barely able to scratch the surface of in this book.

There are stories about transgender women who have created beauty brands, Nikita Dragun's Dragun Beauty, men who have created their own brands, such as Jeffree Star's Jeffree Star Cosmetics, and countless other collaborations with other creators who are also pushing for just as much—more in some cases—inclusion as the founders mentioned in this book. There's so much more to explore with the level of innovation in this industry. In fact, I could probably write an entire book on Fenty Beauty.

However, the following chronologically placed stories show the slow and steady deterioration and redistribution of capital in the beauty industry. We will see product development ranging from category-creators like Beautyblender to Mented Cosmetics, a company focused on producing nude lipsticks for women of color. This shift from "this product does not yet exist" to "the market as it exists today is not addressing the needs of *all* women" happened only because there is now more room for new companies. Having created a path to product popularity that is *not* solely hinged on the support from one of the conglomerates, the earlier companies like Beautyblender, NYX, Huda Beauty, and Tatcha have made it so it is a tiny bit easier for companies like Briogeo, Sol de Janeiro, Live Tinted, and Mented Cosmetics to come about. Do not take this as a sign that the more recent companies had an easy path to success. They absolutely did not—but the booming success of our earlier companies made the later products more enticing to the market.

Without further ado, the following chapters will focus on the stories of:

- Toni Ko's NYX Cosmetics and Bespoke Beauty Brands and her entrepreneurship genes catapulting her beauty career
- Rea Ann Silva's Beautyblender and her rise to fame first as a makeup artist and then as a category creator
- Huda Kattan's Huda Beauty and her obsession with lashes
- Vicky Tsai's Tatcha and her love story with Japanese beauty rituals
- Nancy Twine's Briogeo and her journey with natural hair care products

- Heela Yang and Camila Pierotti's Sol de Janeiro and their ode to Brazilian sunshine
- Deepica Mutyala's Live Tinted and her focus on community-building for brown women everywhere
- And finally, Amanda Johnson and KJ Miller's Mented Cosmetics and the start of nude lipsticks over a bottle of wine

We'll see that it wasn't easy for these women to develop the products and sometimes even more difficult to sell them. Some of these hardships are tangible. Finances, for example, become a big logistical hurdle for many of these women. A lot of the products and the establishment of these companies are self-financed, so of course, we'll see stories of women forgoing salaries for years and years to reinvest in their brand. Some of the hardships are intangible—we'll see stories of women hearing that they are trying to develop products for a beauty standard that people do not aspire to.

We'll also see concrete examples of how the industry is changing. The situation so far is that, although driven by a conglomerate model, the world is changing rapidly. Things are being digitized quicker and in newer ways, e-commerce is becoming a more accessible platform, people have more money to spend on beauty products, inclusion in this industry has suddenly become table stakes, and values-based buying has become an important factor in purchasing behavior. The profiles are written chronologically to show this gradual progression. The companies these women are producing go from innovating through category creation, to introducing a new price point for existing products, to creating entire brands and product lines to service an underrepresented demographic.

I loved hearing these stories, and I love these brands. Getting to talk to some of these women was by far the most rewarding part of writing this book. The messaging of the brands these women have created was as clear in our conversations as they have been in every piece of marketing I've seen so far. A lot of it is wit, intelligence, gumption, industry knowledge, and unparalleled business acumen. It is, however, also in part an unwavering belief in the brands they are creating. These women are smart, passionate, and have taken a lot of risks to get us to a more innovative and more inclusive place with beauty.

I'm proud to spotlight their stories, so here they are.

TONI KO'S NYX COSMETICS AND BESPOKE BEAUTY BRANDS

―――

For most people, success does not just fall into our laps. You have to hustle. Toni Ko hustled to create NYX Professional Makeup in 1999. Toni is the epitome of the American dream. She moved to California from South Korea at a very young age and began seventh grade with only "yes," "no," and "thank you" in her English language arsenal, she said on *The May Lee Show*. For someone who relied solely on her high school ESL classes to learn the language, Toni took advantage of her entrepreneurial instincts to create a company that ended up selling for $500 million to one of the biggest cosmetics conglomerates in the world, *L'Oréal*. More importantly, though, she created a new category for drugstore brands with products that are reliable and high-quality, products that consumers today (like me) know and love and use religiously.

Toni's hankering for creating beauty products didn't just go away after she sold NYX. After the end of a grueling five years of a cosmetics noncompete, Toni founded Bespoke Beauty Brands, a beauty incubator, to help influencers use their social capital to sell products. Once a new student in the world of beauty products, wrote *Forbes'* Clare O'Connor, Toni is now using her decades of knowledge to push innovation and inclusion in this industry forward.

NYX

Born in Daegu, South Korea, Toni moved to Southern California at the age of thirteen with her parents. Her parents ran a successful perfume and cosmetics business first in retail and then as wholesalers, so entrepreneurship and the "learn as you go" attitude were instilled in her at an early age. This attitude, however, sounded a little extreme in Toni's case. In fact, she shared in *Behind Her Empire* that her parents' teaching style had a major influence on her work ethic. Her dad raised her with a spartan mindset, she said, in which only the strongest survive. As she explained to Career Contessa, this Darwinian ideology made her "an extremely mentally and emotionally strong woman who isn't afraid to take risks," leading to the eventual success of her later ventures.

I found Toni's childhood to be quite fascinating. Again, this shocks me, but Toni didn't speak any English as she entered middle school in a new country. I cannot imagine being a preteen in California and going through school without the added support of knowing the language. While everyone else went through the motions of math, gym, science, repeat, Toni spent *FOUR* hours a day in an English language class for her first three years in school. (The May Lee Show) "There's part of me that feels like I got my childhood stolen," Toni said as she recalled her school days spending half her time in a language class.

Eventually, her English improved and she began high school trying to catch up on everything else. She describes herself as a "super awkward" kid and recalls mainly hanging out with the other "awkward" Asian immigrants in her class. "We were all socially awkward together, and we were the outsiders. … The cool kids hung out in the center core, and we hung out in the outer core." With this outer core group of friends, she hung out in the local watering hole for teens in LA, Kmart.

Drawing inspiration from her mom's skin care rituals and routines, she said in *Habits & Hustle*, Toni would walk up and down the aisles of her local Kmart, exploring the product offerings. Despite being in a beauty-forward household, she told *The Korea Herald*, she was not allowed to wear makeup at school, but she loved window-shopping at the department store for the expensive, high-end makeup products.

This really resonated with me. I used to hang out and browse for products at CVS as I waited for the bus, and I'd also think of brands like MAC as the unattainable holy grail product that I would one day, after I'd saved up enough, finally own. Toni felt this too, but instead of just imagining a MAC product finally in her hands, she also saw a gaping hole in the market.

This was the nineties, and there were very few brands compared to today. The three distinct makeup categories that Toni remembers from that time are:

- The older brands, with limited color offerings. Muted tones by Chanel, Estée Lauder, Lancôme, and others.

- The "cool" brands—her words from *Raising the Bar*—that were way above her price range: Stila, Urban Decay, and MAC. Yes, they gave her choices for fun colors, but not if she had to spend that much.
- Lastly, the drugstore brands like Maybelline and L'Oréal, where products weren't always quality made.

There was no in-between brand that would give Toni the color range and variety that she saw in the cool but expensive brands, so she decided to create her own.

The Ko Entrepreneurial Gene

Luckily, alongside her winning attitude bred by her Spartan upbringing was the deep-seated history of entrepreneurship in her family, passed down from her great-grandfather, to her parents, and eventually to her. Through high school and later, Toni worked for her family in their beauty supply store in Los Angeles. She learned the ins and outs of the business, and after she turned twenty-five, she decided that she was ready to take her own venture (Korea Herald).

Toni decided to start NYX in 1999 at the age of twenty-five with a $250,000 loan from her mother as an initial investment. This is important to consider because in addition to almost a decade of experience understanding "another side of business," she told *The Seattle Times*, where the family was selling products to retailers rather than customers, Toni was able to rely on a significant nest egg to finance the initial cost of her company.

I want to emphasize that Toni was extremely lucky to have generational wealth built into her company's initial financing. This does not mean she did not face hardships, but she did get a loan from her mother, a hefty chunk of change that allowed her to rent a small office in LA and start the production of NYX's first two products, eyeliners and lipliners, at $1.99 each. Two dollars in 1999 amounts to $3.14 today, so still a very cheap product and far off from the twenty-dollar price point of MAC products. Let me also say: it's jarring to ever think about NYX cosmetics as a two-product brand because those who know it today know that NYX cosmetics has about a *million* products.

Growth of NYX

Toni began NYX with those two products because she understood the needs of the industry. She also knew that a majority of expenses for beauty companies come from marketing budgets, not from manufacturing. Knowing this allowed Toni to focus on investing any and all revenue for the first few years back into wholesale product purchasing to maintain NYX's low prices (Career Contessa). For marketing, she was "confident that if [she] sold a high-quality product at a really great price point, [her] consumers would do all the marketing for [her]" through the age-old technique of word-of-mouth recommendations.

Toni "wore every hat and served in every position and department" at NYX in her first year and did not take a salary for the first three years. She instead reinvested every dollar she made back into the business. Despite being the company's only employee, she made $2 million in sales in the first year, paying her mother back for the $250,000 investment and then some.

NYX started scaling up as Toni worked tirelessly to expose the brand at trade shows (Habits & Hustle). Relying on her frugal business model, which some may now call a "lean startup" strategy, Toni DIY-ed the transportation for the trade shows, packing everything herself and driving back and forth to save on hotel costs. This persisted throughout NYX's first few years as Toni continued wearing the many hats, sometimes even answering her own phone pretending to be the receptionist. Despite this, the exposure she got at trade shows helped her grow her retail customer base and eventually gave NYX international exposure (Career Contessa).

Toni has described herself as someone who is not a "natural-born salesperson" and insists that NYX products sold themselves (The May Lee Show). Over ten years in a successful and financially viable operation, Toni expanded the NYX product line to include lipsticks and other eye products, as the company was on a steady rise when another breakthrough came in early 2008.

Resilient NYX

The year 2008 marked a negative turning point for many businesses. The global financial crisis contributed to the downfall of some of the world's most powerful companies, but the recession actually helped accelerate NYX's standing from being a business-to-business company to finally engaging the consumer side of commerce.

The Lipstick Effect, according to Investopedia, is the idea that consumers are still willing to spend money on small indulgences, despite financial hardships. This phenomenon rang true for NYX and catapulted Toni's business. This does not work for every makeup company; however, customers looking for a low-cost, high emotional return opportunity to indulge in makeup uniquely benefited NYX because it was a much cheaper brand and therefore easier to justify the purchase.

NYX continued to gain traction through the financial crisis and eventually became a household name for quality drugstore products, according to *CSQ*. While the products were already selling well in local boutique stores, Toni brought in a minority investor in 2009 to help her get connected to retailers like Target and Walgreens, transforming the business into the national phenomenon it is today.

Toni often talks about how she doesn't have many memories from her NYX days, that she was "constantly living out of a suitcase… working nonstop but felt like I had nothing to show for it." Spearheading a multimillion-dollar company from conception to sale is not "nothing," but Toni was "suddenly tired of it all and just felt ready" to exit the business.

Having dedicated half of her life to NYX, Toni decided to sell the company to L'Oréal for an estimated $500 million in July 2014. In an *Inc.* article, "What I Did the Day After Selling My Company," Toni talked about how she worked to successfully prepare for a seamless transition, set up a team to run the day-to-day operations independently, and was finally able to "have work-life balance" for once.

Life After NYX Is Perverse

Toni soon realized that there is no work-life balance without work, and she was dazed and confused on day one of unemployment. She slept for twelve hours the day after NYX sold. As she searched for something to pass the time, she thought, "How many days can you spend on the beach? How many times can you go shopping?" It didn't take her too long to stop being "bored out of [her] mind" and get to her next venture, a sunglasses company called Perverse.

Perverse, which launched two years after NYX sold, did not turn out to be hugely successful, and Toni struggled with the business (Behind Her Empire). Her mistake was her assumption that because she loves sunglasses, loves collecting them, and could see a viable market for selling them at a fraction of market prices, that her level of familiarity with the sector would make her business successful. Turns out, that is not the only necessary skill set, and Toni describes this time as "another form of learning experiences," taking away a few key lessons:

1. You have to understand your sales channels.
2. You have to know and love your manufacturers.
3. You have to be intimately familiar with your company operations (know your finance/HR/all other teams *well*).

Perverse is still operational as Thomas James LA, and after her not-so-lucrative experience with this company, Toni patiently waited for her five-year noncompete with NYX to expire, and she counted down the days until she was able to dip her feet back into what she knows best: the beauty industry.

Bespoke Beauty Brands

This was Toni's big idea to get back into beauty—using her resources, contacts, and industry knowledge, she wanted to create a platform/think tank/incubator, a one-stop-shop resource for others to follow suit and make their impression on the world of beauty. In 2019, likely the second her noncompete expired, Toni started a venture capital firm, Butter Ventures, and an incubator, Bespoke Beauty Brands, to act as an accelerator for up-and-coming brands to help bring affordable color cosmetics into the beauty industry (Cosmetics Design). According to Coveteur, she's funded more than twelve female-founded brands, ranging from a CBD brand called Sagely to a Botox bar brand called Alchemy 43, actively helping shape the future of beauty.

Through Bespoke Beauty Brands, Toni set standards high with their first line with Kim Chi, the Instagram sensation who gained her claim to fame on *RuPaul's Drag Race*. Toni's financial investment on ventures like KimChi Chic Beauty enables her to tactfully share equity, stocks, and board membership while relying on the influencers to sell products organically (CSQ). In fact, for KimChi Chic Beauty, social media supporters accounted for a whopping 92 percent of their sales. Relying on the same frugal marketing that made NYX so popular, Toni is using social media to catapult Bespoke Beauty Brand companies into commercial success.

It's clear from Toni's latest ventures where she sees the future of the beauty industry going. She sees it as an environment where social media drives sales, and she sees a real opportunity for differentiation in the branding and products available. She is encouraged by the "many young, female entrepreneurs now running companies. Before, it was all L'Oréal, Revlon, Coty—all these male-dominated companies. But there are so many other brands now run by women taking over. I'm really amazed and proud of these changes that we've made" (Coveteur).

She also recognizes that "real innovation comes from storytelling" (CSQ). We'll see this to be true time and time again with other companies in this book (particularly Tatcha) and the importance and true value of a good and authentic story. There are so many examples of companies, some in this book, where the founders are reticent to involve investors because the story of the brand will get tarnished by solely focusing on financial growth. For Toni, because the products are sold through stories and connections people have with the influencers, the story isn't in the product itself; "it's in the way it's told online through social media or YouTube."

Toni and the Future

Toni is not sitting back. She is actively contributing to innovation in this industry through her incubator and her venture capital efforts to fund other $500 million ideas. We'll see other examples in this book of companies passively serving as points of inspiration for up-and-coming entrepreneurs. Rooshy Roy founded AAVRANI by looking at Vicky Tsai's success with Tatcha and saying, "If she can do it, so can I."

Toni, on the other hand, is putting money on being a point of inspiration through her investments. Toni's commitment and Bespoke Beauty Brand's support for promoting products from people like Kim Chi and Jason Wu indicates her intention to keep supporting creators in the East Asian community. I am so looking forward to whom she works with next.

I follow Toni on Instagram, and she is still a Spartan entrepreneur through and through. She sold NYX for $500 million, and she still lives the life of an A-to-Z entrepreneur. She still gets her hands dirty with the nitty-gritty bits of the business. I once saw on an Instagram story she posted of herself packing boxes for Jason Wu's makeup line. I thought to myself, *Why doesn't she just pay someone to do that for her?*

REA ANN SILVA'S BEAUTYBLENDER

———

Ironically shaped like a tear drop, even though all it does is *solve* problems, Beautyblender is a holy grail product for makeup application. The genius behind this sponge is Rea Ann Silva, and it all started during her time as a professional makeup artist. While using a bulky and expensive technique called airbrushing to apply foundation for TV and movie stars, Rea Ann realized nothing worked as well as the Beautyblender she had fashioned for herself by cutting a sponge into the iconic teardrop shape.

She made more of these teardrop sponges as they started disappearing wherever Rea Ann brought them with her. She recalled, in a *Business Insider* article, "It was like they sprouted legs and walked away off set, and I realized people were stealing them." Eventually, people started paying for these DIY sponges. Rea Ann worked with a manufacturer to produce the Beautyblender we know today, and the product revolutionized the beauty industry, selling over fifty million pieces since its inception, as reported by Insider.

Faked It Till She Made It

Rea Ann grew up in Calabasas, California, and, she said on *Breaking Beauty*, had an "unremarkable childhood" where her mother, "a naturalist," was a waitress and her father was an auto mechanic at a Ford factory. Rea Ann's early memories of beauty were similar to Toni's—exploring the products in drugstores while her mom shopped for other products. She recalled, "I didn't look like any of the models that were used to advertise cosmetics at the time, and there was this very aspirational look of beauty and what beauty meant to you. So I'd get excited by those images and then look in the mirror and go, 'Wait, I don't look like them; how do I translate this to myself?'"

Throughout her childhood, Rea Ann was exposed to a wide spectrum of makeup through her Latinx heritage. On an Instagram video, she talked about how she was exposed to Latina women who were embracing and enhancing their natural features through makeup, and women on Telenovelas who wanted to show off their glamour. This range not only helped Rea Ann develop ideas of how to push boundaries with makeup but also showed her "everything from minimalist to maximalist."

While Rea Ann was interested in pursuing beauty, she first chose to go the fashion route because it was a more democratized industry. Not everyone wears makeup, but everyone does wear clothes. She decided to enroll in the Fashion Institute of Design & Merchandising (FIDM) in Los Angeles as one of the first students at the school. Being at FIDM in the eighties, Rea Ann said in a Stacye Branché interview that her eventual goal was to live out the fashion designer fantasy of traveling the world. Crystal Moten, in "The Woman Behind Beautyblender," writes that through her school years and under the mentorship of the late Professor Nancy Riegelman, Rea Ann got increasingly interested in fashion illustration, sketching, color, and texture, and she developed skills that eventually helped boost her skills as a makeup artist.

Despite her schooling, Rea Ann, having recently become a single mother, ended up in a part-time job to support herself through college as a perfume model, which she describes as "the worst job because nobody likes you; nobody wants to be sprayed with perfume" (Breaking Beauty). As sad as it is to be in a job where people actively avoid you, her department store job did introduce Rea Ann to the cohort of makeup artists and creative enthusiasts around the makeup counter (Branché).

Fueled by her love for beauty, she decided to move to a job at the makeup counter, where she realized that she needed to quickly learn how to "upsell multiple products because there's not one color for somebody like me." She found that the other Latinx customers were gravitating toward her for product recommendations. Through her work at department store counters, she not only ended up developing contacts in this field, but she also became a "mixologist when it came to complexion... specializing in doing makeup for celebrities and women of color because there really was a very small niche group of artists who specialized in this area."

"I faked it till I made it," says Rea Ann, as she put together a portfolio of her work and continued to gain traction in the makeup artistry world (Branché). At this time, there weren't a lot of well-known schools for makeup or beauty, so her experience came from the work she was doing. She built her portfolio and client base by word of mouth and networking. At first, she'd offer up her services for free to the never-ending group of models and photographers, who were more than happy to have her on set if it meant they didn't have to pay for makeup work. She worked hard, with the inspiration partly coming from her parents' work ethic and partly from the necessity of needing to support her child (National Museum of American History). Rea Ann eventually built a portfolio big enough to get an agent who helped further her connections to celebrities in the music industry (Breaking Beauty).

Giving out free work and building a client base was not easy, especially in the eighties and nineties, and particularly for a Latina single mother. It does not surprise me one bit that Rea Ann faced discrimination throughout her career because, unfortunately, that is the standard experience of people of color in most industries. She said that she had directors who refused to work with her and often found herself defending her resume even with twenty-five years of experience in the industry (National Museum of American History).

I don't want to call it lucky that she faced discrimination; it's not a positive experience. However, because her access to clients was often limited, she was able to build a niche client base working with entertainers of color. Because of the limited availability of beauty products at the time, Rea Ann was very used to mixing shades to match her own skin tone and became well known for her ability to work with different colors, textures, and generally with enhancing the natural beauty of people of color (Dickerson).

This unique skill set led her to opportunities working on MTV with Whitney Houston, Tupac, Sean "Diddy" Combs, Biggie Smalls, and other artists of color. Eventually, she was able to build her portfolio with this specialty and learned very early on how to mix foundation shades to find the perfect match for people with darker skin tones (Breaking Beauty). In an episode of *The Make Down*, I learned that Rea

Ann made a name for herself in this industry and worked a lot with F. Gary Gray, extremely well-known filmmaker and music video director, who included her in his film, *Friday*, which became her first feature work.

Born Out of Necessity

If you remember TV in the early 2000s, *Girlfriends* was a hugely popular show for which Rea Ann happened to be a makeup artist. *Girlfriends* was a show that broke a lot of barriers. According to *USA Today*, it was the first ensemble sitcom focusing on the lives of four Black women, and it was one of the first shows to tackle the narratives of Black women firsthand. Technically, and most relevant for Rea Ann, it was also "the very first show shot in high-def, and suddenly, in HD, you were able to see every pore; you were able to see every bump," and so she needed to find a way to achieve an airbrushed, natural look (The Make Down).

One of the most popular makeup techniques that existed at the time was airbrushing. This technique involved using a sprayer to apply foundation. The airbrush creates an even surface of foundation across the skin, resulting in an even, natural-looking skin tone. It was, however, cumbersome to carry. Not everyone knew how to use the tool, and it was really impractical to move around on set, especially one with four lead actresses.

As a result, Beautyblender was "born out of necessity." The four lead actresses on *Girlfriends* ended up being Rea Ann's test subjects as she used triangular wedges to apply makeup. Instead of using them as is, she cut them up, round on the bottom and pointy on top, to better blend the makeup and created the shape of what we know as Beautyblenders today (Insider).

After ten years of experience in the beauty industry, Rea Ann's initial version of Beautyblender worked well. In a conversation with Necessite, Rea Ann said she started selling her DIY version, Beautyblender 1.0, which made her enough to use the revenue as supplemental income. She was selling the product to other makeup artists, initially assuming they would use it in the same vein that she did—in their professional work. She soon realized that makeup professionals were using the product, yes, but they were also gifting them to friends and family. Could this be a product that could have commercial success beyond the industry?

To explore this, Rea Ann began doing her own market research to develop her product at a larger scale. Her research technique was simple yet highly effective. She would go to drugstores to browse for makeup and pay close attention to where they were being manufactured (Breaking Beauty). She realized that the industry was quite incestuous. There are only a limited number of manufacturers, and she ended up coming across the sole manufacturer of all sponges.

During the product development phase, she was protective of the end result. She wanted to ensure this sponge was different, more reliable, and easier to use than the triangle wedges that were on the market. She also wanted it to be a product that was reusable and, therefore, sustainable and environmentally friendly (The Make Down). The manufacturers sent her sample after sample, all with the teardrop shape with different colors to mark the different materials they used (Breaking Beauty).

Through this iterative process, out came a pink teardrop sponge as her sample. It was simply an initial rendering that was likely made out of leftover hot pink sponge that was going to waste anyway. She remembered, during a segment on *The Drew Barrymore Show*, that she got a sample box from the manufacturers of a set of sponges, prefaced with a note in red that said "DON'T LOOK AT THE COLOR!" and saw that it was the brightest pink. She thought, *This is the perfect color because I'm revolutionizing this tool that I think everybody needs to have, and I need people to see it from across the room.* It worked; every time I go to a Sephora, the pink sponge is the first thing I see.

Beautyblender finally launched after four years of this back-and-forth process. According to *WorkParty*, Beautyblender initially operated out of a small editing studio in Rea Ann's garage, with her daughter, Erica Dickerson, helping with assembly and other odd jobs. Erica also focused on content development for Beautyblender and helped establish the brand identity early on by producing and following influencers who were first starting out on YouTube.

In fact, Erica was the first Beautyblender model "because I was free... literally free of charge and available," she said. Being the face of the brand so early on meant that an Afro Latina woman would be their representative woman, immediately establishing a voice and a face to the Beautyblender brand.

Pivot

The beginning of Beautyblender marked slow growth for the company. Rea Ann was still working as a makeup artist, finding it really tough to focus on her business with such a wide portfolio of clients (WorkParty). Beautyblender was also the first product in its category; no one had heard of it before, so it needed a lot of hand-holding to introduce people to its use case and reliability. While at first Rea Ann was only selling to fellow professional makeup artists, she slowly expanded the sales channels to include retailers.

Despite the slow financial growth of the company, she appreciated this slow start. She's often referred to time as a helpful way for her to step into building a brand and category of makeup because "ignorance is bliss," she said to *Insider*, and thought she may never have taken the first step toward creating this product if she knew what a daunting project it would end up becoming (Insider). "For me," she recalled, "what worked for Beautyblender was the curation of the brand. The fact that it took longer to get acknowledgment let me build a strong foundation for the brand before growing." Even at this comfortable pace, Rea Ann was having a hard time pivoting from a makeup artist mindset to a business mindset. "All of these things were a totally different language to me," she said (WorkParty).

At this point, the company was meant to help out with her kids' college fund and maybe provide supplemental income, she said to *Daily Mail*, but the business soon outgrew Rea Ann's garage. As YouTube was growing to become a medium for reviews, beauty tips, and the next innovative thing, Beautyblender used vloggers and celebrity fans to help add "credibility and endorsement to a product that truly delivered results" (Daily Mail).

Today, Beautyblender is a massive company and a household name. It's even used to describe the many copycats that have tried and failed to produce the products. "Imitation is the most sincere form of flattery," Rea Ann says in response to having many, *many* imitators. She maintains that being the creator of a category is worth more to her than being the only one in the category (WorkParty).

Imitation worked for some, but no one was able to match the proprietary formula of Beautyblender. Rea Ann maintains the product formula—the makeup of the product, if you will—still remains exclusive to Beautyblenders, partially because of her close relationship with the manufacturers in Pennsylvania. Sephora was one of the initial imitators, and despite their many tries, their own version failed to match the obsession that Beautyblender had garnered. Because of this unmatched potential, *Beauty Independent* notes that Sephora became interested in being a distributor for Beautyblender, thereby expanding the products' reach, name recognition, and revenue stream.

Bounce Foundation

Since its inception, Beautyblender's product line has expanded to include concealers, foundation, and products beyond the little pink sponge. Learning opportunities are still coming to Rea Ann and the team as the launch of their foundation line, Bounce, fell short of forty shades, which caused a lot of backlash. This is partly what I describe as values-based buying. Despite Rea Ann being a color expert and having a keen understanding of what consumers need, the fact that the foundation line was anything short of forty shades was a deal-breaker for many of her consumers. More specifically, *Refinery29* notes that consumers found it "disappointing, pointing out the unrealistic orange-y colors, and assailing the brand for the shortage of dark shade options."

This standard came partly from the aforementioned global success of Fenty Beauty. Although it's arguable whether companies that have forty shades are any more or less inclusive than those who do not—what if twenty-five of your forty shades are all lighter shades?

Beautyblender was able to weather the storm by expanding its product line with eight new shades, which was the plan all along. It took as long as it did to get the shades out there because "it's harder to differentiate undertones in darker shades." This meant that the tan and dark shades required some extra love and attention. The darkest shade developed then was beyond Sephora's darkest available color at the time. Rea Ann has assured her customers that they are not done creating new shades; "there are an infinite amount of skin tones in the world, and we will continue to innovate and develop."

Beautyblender Today

Erica has taken on the role of global beauty director and CEO in training. She educates consumers about Beautyblender's products, she tells the story of the brand, she champions her Black/Latina heritage, and she shouts from the rooftops that Beautyblender is founded by a Latina single mom (Work-Party). Erica's goal is to continuously "champion inclusivity in everything that we do, whether that is the influencers that we are hiring and using our posts that we are sharing, down to the people we want to employ."

According to *POPSUGAR*, seventeen Beautyblender applicators are sold every minute, and Rea Ann still maintains 100 percent control of the company while working as a professional makeup artist (if booked *months* in advance) because she loves the trade. She also has a Smithsonian exhibit titled *The Only One in the Room*, aptly and particularly named so because she has been "the only one in the room at many different points of [her] life" (National Museum of American History).

Rea Ann started off in the background of Beautyblender; she isn't used to talking about who she is as a founder. Her name isn't on the product she created; it's not "Rea Ann's Beautyblender," and the nature of her work as a makeup artist often required her to stay anonymous and confidential. She now says, "It would've been helpful for people to know about my background and my career when I launched my first cosmetic product" (Beauty Independent).

This has since changed. Today, she calls her company Rea. deeming Beauty, Inc. as her product line expands beyond Beautyblenders. She is very much at the forefront of her company Instagram page, and she is very much in the spotlight, proudly and loudly telling us that she is the Latina behind Beautyblender.

HUDA KATTAN'S
HUDA BEAUTY

———

"You don't belong here." Hearing this would cause anyone to have a visceral reaction, and so was the case for Huda Kattan, beauty phenomenon and founder and CEO of Huda Beauty. Huda's reaction *was* visceral; she decided to run far away from the world of finance and start her career doing what she always wanted to do: play with makeup.

Fast-forward several years later. Huda found fame through her blog, HudaBeauty.com, and through it, an avenue to create a $1.2 billion beauty empire. In an interview with *Girlboss Radio*, Huda talked about how she capitalized on her skills as a leader and an entrepreneur, a missing piece of the beauty market, a community in Dubai willing to experiment with new products, and support from her two sisters who helped her jumpstart Huda Beauty. Since then, Huda has become one of the most followed personalities on Instagram, leading her products to global fame with forty-eight million followers, all without showing any signs of stopping.

Southern Girl

In a *Bustle* interview, Huda describes herself as a "Southern girl," born in Oklahoma and raised in Tennessee. She was bullied in school when she was younger and described having a "rough childhood growing up as an Arab American in the United States. She also told *Entrepreneur Middle East* that throughout her childhood, she suffered from a self-diagnosed "ugly child syndrome," when really she just looked a little different from all the other kids around her.

Constantly hearing that you don't belong and that you don't look good sticks with you. As a result of being surrounded by people, ads, and media that perpetuated this idea of exclusion, Huda became very concerned with what others thought of her. In doing so, she began using beauty as a tool for transformation, she told *Vogue Arabia*, and even at a young age, she became a makeup mogul in her house. She grew up comfortably familiar with beauty products first introduced to her by her sister, Alya, and her first and favorite beauty product, because she was a hairy kid, were tweezers. She said in one of her YouTube videos, "My makeup business story!" that she got very good at using tweezers, and "by the time she was fourteen, she was sculpting her sister's eyebrows."

It's very strange to think about a fourteen-year-old who is good at doing eyebrows. I really admire this talent, maybe because my parents own eyebrow threading salons in New York City, and I know how hard it is to get the shape right. And as a hairy person myself, I have ruined my own eyebrows many times, trying to tweeze just one more strand of hair. Huda clearly had talent even as a young kid for understanding the way facial features could be shaped—a skill that would catapult her business to success much later.

Despite the fact that Huda enjoyed playing with makeup from a young age, she didn't necessarily see beauty as a career path for herself. Since she came from a Middle Eastern family, the expectation was for her "to be a doctor, or something kind of 'serious,'" she recalled (Huda Beauty). Keeping these ambitions in mind, Huda was determined to take on a more "serious" path during college, where she graduated with a degree in finance. Like many of the stories highlighted in this book, her eventual goal was to get an MBA and establish a successful career in finance.

Like many who pick a field they don't actually want to study, Huda spent her undergraduate years confused about what she wanted to do, all the while realizing in the back of her mind that finance was not it. Deciding to go all in on the "serious" path of finance but maintain the "people" side of things, she decided to work as a recruiter in the industry (Girlboss Radio). Despite years of exposure to the work, the field itself ended up rejecting her as she was eventually let go by a mean boss who told Huda she didn't belong in finance.

HudaBeauty.com

Having been pushed out of the world of finance, Huda tapped into the love she had for beauty when she was a kid. She realized that was what she really wanted to be doing and began to study makeup artistry at the Joe Blasco Makeup Academy. Through this work, she finally realized the value of investing her time in something she truly loved (Girlboss Radio). With a financial crisis looming, her sister gave her a not-so-subtle nudge to get started in beauty. What better time to try something new?

In "How I became a makeup mogul," Huda talks about how her headfirst dive into makeup pushed her to start HudaBeauty.com in 2010. This blog was meant to be a way to share her "experience and tips as a makeup artist, but it was also a way to inspire others who felt like [her] and didn't see anyone who looked like [her] in the media," she said to *Glamour*. She wanted everyone to feel welcome as part of the beauty world, and she used the blog as a playground to experiment with new looks.

Huda's blog is really one of the defining factors of how her makeup career succeeded. It turns out there was (and still is) a surprisingly large group of people who didn't feel like they belonged, who did not fit into the beauty standards created and perpetuated by society. There was an audience ripe for the taking. Huda's willingness to talk about her body hair, her eyebrow routine, and the way she looked and felt different when she put on makeup really resonated with her fan base. Not only was Huda new to the beauty industry, but the concept of a brown girl blogging about makeup was also new. I've been watching YouTube makeup videos and following bloggers for a long time, and even in my diverse repertoire of favorite YouTubers, only recently has the pool become more representative of Asian and Middle Eastern women.

Not only was HudaBeauty.com's content new to the internet world, but it was also very innovative and experimental. The digital world was still emerging in 2010, and people were being exposed to new ways of wearing makeup, which her audience was dying to see. Huda just so happened to fulfill this demand. "I will put almost anything on my face, and I will try any procedure, and people are interested that we're going to show them something new" (Girlboss Radio). Slowly but surely, her audience grew. Huda continued to push and filled her schedule as a makeup artist to gain new followers and expand the audience for her blog.

Dubai

Huda used Facebook to increase HudaBeauty.com's global exposure. She relied on these channels to gain traction in another market in the Middle East. It just so happened that the beauty industry in the Middle East also had a hankering for innovative work and a need to push the envelope with makeup.

While still working as a makeup artist, Huda's blog was taking off alongside her incredibly demanding schedule of makeup in the morning, content production during the day, and events at night so she could meet people and share her trade (*all* while she was pregnant). She repeated this routine every day until her blog began gaining serious traction.

Huda's daughter was born when her blog was *just* taking off, and she maintained her grasp on this work as she was falling asleep with Nour in her arms and grappled with an age-old choice: "you could either be a mom or a career woman" (Bustle). Despite her newfound responsibilities, Huda, encouraged by her other sister Mona, decided to act on a clearly missing piece of the market and launched a lash line through a new brand, Huda Beauty. She did so because, as she writes on Huda Beauty's website, she "wasn't satisfied with the style and quality of lashes that were available at the time, so I often ended up stacking and customizing the lashes myself to suit the client's eye shape."

The original version of the lashes was not the perfectly wispy ones we know today. The original Huda Beauty lashes were DIY-ed from dollar-store lashes that Huda would then fashion to have the classic full volume, wispy length, and flick at the end. With a $6,500 investment from her family, according to *Breaking Beauty*, backed by the clearly promising content on her blog, Huda took these lashes to Sephora Dubai, and, to her surprise, they said yes.

Needless to say, the lashes sold well—so well, in fact, they sold a year's worth of supply in just one week, giving Huda the financial investment she needed to move toward a proper manufacturing channel. The manufacturing process for Huda, once she graduated from dollar-store DIY, was extremely precise. "Reduce one millimeter here, add a piece there," said Huda as she took on the role of CEO. She wanted to keep the company innovative, but she was also very protective about the quality and precision of her lashes. The success of her blog proved she had an instinct for understanding the market, and she wanted to make sure that this knowledge seeped into every product the company would develop (Girlboss Radio).

Huda Beauty grew significantly after its inception, and Huda eventually realized that the growth she envisioned for her company was not possible with *just* her gritty and scrappy attitude and industry know-how. She needed more capital to be better at experimenting, to have more room to play with products, and to ensure true mentorship and growth opportunities for those working for her. To think beyond what existed, her team needed real product development, PR, and data strategy, and Huda's gut instincts were no longer going to cut it in this incredibly competitive market.

Huda Beauty was a relatively well-known brand by 2017 and was, therefore, able to catch the eye of a firm like TSG Consumer Partners. TSG Consumer Partners has invested in companies like CorePower, ZOEVA, e.l.f. cosmetics, and IT Cosmetics—the big wigs. In fact, TSG Consumer Partners was particularly interested in Huda Beauty because of its "disruptive, next-generation approach toward consumer outreach and product." Together, TSG and Huda are planning to broaden the distribution of the products beyond specialty retail and e-commerce. Maybe we'll start seeing Huda Beauty pop-up stores!

Number Forty-Seven

Today, Huda Kattan sits comfortably at number forty-seven on *Forbes* America's Self-Made Women with a net worth of $510 million (*Forbes*). Huda wants to keep pushing the envelope, changing the face of beauty and sharing the message that beauty is about power and confidence. This is very true for me and is likely true for other women. I absolutely feel more powerful and confident when I put 10 percent more effort into the way I look on the day of a big presentation.

Huda found a way to tap into this makeup-driven confidence not only in her messaging but also in the way she presents her products. "Promotion Day," "Board Meeting," "Trendsetter," and "Icon" are just four of her best-selling lip products. When I see these names and the way she's branding her products, I see the profile of women who pick up this lipstick and use it as a bold statement of confidence. Huda often talks about how, if she was having a bad day, she would go out and buy lipstick to make herself feel better, and her emphasis on deriving power and confidence from a bold lip and a bold personality is reflected in her products.

Huda's wildest dream, she shared with *Business of Fashion*, is for her company to be the next Estée Lauder. She doesn't want Huda Beauty to "be just a big brand; we want to be the biggest brand." She also wants Huda Beauty to be responsible not only for doing what they already do, pushing the envelope and creating bold products, but for the creation and creativity that comes from being backed by the financial prowess of a giant beauty conglomerate. This is an interesting dynamic to consider for a company like Huda Beauty. Despite companies like hers disrupting the conglomerate-driven product development in this industry, there is still interest in being one of them. Huda Beauty has catapulted so significantly and in such a short amount of time, and with Huda's own popularity added into the mix, Huda Beauty could easily be the next Estée Lauder.

This is one of the main reasons that Huda's journey has been on a familiar track but still off the beaten path. Huda's popularity on Instagram and the uniqueness of her content have allowed her to take an almost reality star approach to running her business. She has her own show on Facebook TV, *Huda Boss*, and has more followers than any of the other founders in this book. If her company goes public, Huda will be an unstoppable force in this industry. Given that she already has a skin care line, Wishful, and a fragrance line, Kayali, under her belt, Huda Beauty is very likely to have the capital to become the next Estée Lauder.

Huda Today

The story of Huda Beauty and Huda's experience with the transformative power of makeup still rings true. Creating her products with attention to detail and true purpose, Huda "is not motivated by money, so the bottom line does not matter. … It is about giving people the power to then express who they want to be no matter who they are or where they are from" (Huda Beauty). Of course, it's much easier to say that money does not matter when your company is growing as rapidly as Huda Beauty has. However, it's clear from her messaging, her social media presence, and the products that have come out of Huda Beauty that she has always been about blazing the trail. The original value that buyers saw in Huda's products, which does include quality and diversity, is still prevalent in what the company produces, and this type of values-based commerce continues to play a role in the company's success.

Yes, inclusion has been a big part of her work because her own lived experiences have been shaped by the lack of inclusion in the products she had access to growing up. Huda offers nude lipsticks that cater to many different skin tones, and her #FauxFilter Foundations have a wide range of colors and a conscious formula to, as a review on *High Life North* said, not "look ashy on the skin," and there is more than one shade of translucent powders (not just a white powder).

It's also clear, though, that innovation has been the primary driver of her products, and inclusion has largely been a byproduct of this innovation. When asked if her background and childhood spent not fitting in contributed to the ethos of her company, she responded, "I didn't really realize it at the time. Now, yes. At the time when we were starting the brand, it was more I felt it was filling a void for me. And I definitely felt at the time it was that I wanted something different. Whether that was products… maybe later on down the line, a movement" (*Glamour*).

In a video, "Why I'm no longer CEO at Huda Beauty," Huda Kattan talks through the whirlwind that was the last ten years of her life. The past few years have forced her to take a pause and think about where she is in life and how much she's enjoyed being on the consumer side. She told *Harper's Bazaar Arabia* that she enjoys creating content, which was her passion since day one of HudaBeauty.com, the blog, so she decided to appoint Nathalie Kristo as the CEO of Huda Beauty. I read Nathalie's Cosmetic Executive Women profile. She is smart, she's experienced, and she's catapulted Huda Beauty's presence into new markets, including the launch of Wishful in 2019. Huda can now contribute as chairwoman, founder, idea woman, content creator, innovator, and spokeswoman for the power of beauty. She can now do what she always wanted to do—play with makeup.

VICKY TSAI'S TATCHA

———

Born from chaos, skin care company Tatcha is Vicky Tsai's love letter to Japan. As founder and chief treasure hunter (her words), Vicky has grown a business that started in the corner of her parents' garage to what is now a thriving company. According to *Allure*, the company became so successful that Unilever bought Tatcha in 2019 for an estimated $500 million.

Vicky was introduced to the marvel of Japanese beauty through an archaic process. As described by Visit Kanazawa, Japanese craftspeople use layers of hammering paper to make gold leaves. Meanwhile, Kyoto's geisha, and eventually Vicky, used the otherwise-wasted hammering paper as blotting paper to mattify and remove oil from their skin. During a time when Asian beauty was not the aspirational look most companies wanted to invest in, Vicky found a way to fight through the rubble of rejection and bankruptcy for an opportunity to tell the story of how she found authenticity and purity in Japanese beauty rituals and eventually founded Tatcha.

The Chaos

I got a glimpse of Vicky's childhood in an *Inc.* article titled "What Helped Her Build a $500 Million Asian-Beauty Brand." Vicky is the child of Taiwanese immigrants and was born and raised in Houston. "Right away, I became aware that there was one standard of beauty that I would never fit into," she recalled. Her mother owned a beauty store that carried Western skin care brands; "at home, however, she would mix herbs and create more traditional Chinese remedies." Vicky grew up being more drawn to the expensive Western products rather than the home remedies that were part of her heritage. Today, she recognizes that these preferences likely stemmed from her own internal desire to fit in.

The story of Tatcha really begins in 2001, when New Yorkers—and the broader United States—experienced one of the most chaotic and traumatizing days in recent history. Vicky was a trader for Merrill Lynch at the time and spent September 11, 2001, horrifically close to Ground Zero. She described intently on *How I Built This* that she felt the first rumble, then the second boom, and ran out of the building in heels to see utter chaos. She had lost sight of her husband, but eventually, they both made it to their West Village home safely.

Vicky recalled in a *Hello Sunshine* article, "If work is how I spend most of the working hours of my life, it should have meaning." She wanted to change the course of her career, so she began attending Harvard Business School in 2005 and worked as an intern at a big beauty care company, where her job was to conduct hands-on market research, which is fancy business speak for spending her days trying all kinds of products, which ended up giving her acute dermatitis from exposure to the myriad unfamiliar chemicals.

Vicky finished business school and moved on to a brand management position at Starbucks, working tirelessly to meet her demanding travel and workload to launch Frappuccinos in China (NPR). Her job was incredibly demanding—traveling to Asia twice a month to launch a product in just eighteen months, about half the time normally allotted to this task, all without much guidance. Despite having far exceeded the expectations for this job, when she received her performance review, it read "meets expectations."

Frustrated with this underwhelming feedback, Vicky left the role, and soon after, she was recruited to help with a product launch and marketing strategy for Good Guide, a company that was at the forefront of creating a values-based purchasing system. Vicky was there for four months, and the experience of trying to build this business from scratch took a negative toll as she became "increasingly impatient with spending the hours of [her] waking life doing things that [she] didn't believe in." She left her job without a plan B.

Vicky in Japan

There she was, unemployed, disillusioned, and looking for a new path forward. *I've really made a mess for myself,* she thought toward the end of 2008, with the world going into a recession and her own $600,000 in debt. "I felt like I didn't believe in anything anymore," she said, and when she reached that level of apathy, she searched desperately to find meaning in the decisions she had made thus far. While she worked a few jobs to make ends meet, she'd always wanted to spend some time traveling and thought to herself, *Why not now?*

Vicky traveled all over the world. She went to Europe and eventually made her way to Kyoto, where she became very intrigued by Japan's history. Anyone who has been to Kyoto knows it is a city rich with history and culture. Kyoto is also the heart of Japan's geisha world, particularly the area of Gion, where I spent many of my study-abroad days.

Vicky was awestruck by her first encounter with a geisha on the streets of Kyoto. Battling the ups and downs of stress and painful acute dermatitis for years, Vicky could not help but ask the Geisha she met about their skin care rituals. She learned that Japanese rituals and the delicate way in which Geisha take care of their skin have a very astute mind-body connection, where life is "carried out in a series of rituals that bring meaning to the mundane within our days," she told *Travel + Leisure*.

Enamored by the delicacy and efficacy of geisha skincare, she was particularly intrigued by the blotting paper they use that comes from the aforementioned Kanazawa technique. She was intrigued by this masterful use of what would otherwise go to waste and was instantly interested in learning more, so she went to see where these gold leaves were made (NPR). She described the setting during her first encounter with the technique of Kanazawa as "gold everywhere, there's gold on their eyelashes, there's gold on their clothes."

Enchanted by the history, authenticity, and beauty of her experience with geisha and Kanazawa, Vicky had an idea to sell these blotting papers back home in the United States. She impulse-bought ten thousand sheets and financed this purchase by putting her engagement ring on consignment. She had a vision for sharing her treasure trove with other women who were looking for safety and beauty in their products and decided to start a company with the blotting paper as her first product.

Starting Tatcha

It was 2009, and Vicky started Tatcha by financing the upfront expenditures herself. It was a heavy lift that furthered her debt, but she had seen the growth-focused nature of venture capitalism and private equity affect the authenticity of products during her time in the world of finance, and she wanted to protect Tatcha from the revenue-hungry nature of this decision. If she wanted to share the beauty of what she had found and maintain its integrity and simplicity, she was determined to nurture the growth of her brand herself.

Self-financing for Vicky meant working four jobs, begging her landlord for a discount on rent in exchange for maintenance work in the building, selling her valued items, relying on her husband's poker skills for day-to-day expenses, and putting all her dreams on multiple credit cards. The beginning of Tatcha marked something exciting, but it was also a financially daunting time for Vicky, who was nine months pregnant at the time

Vicky wanted to grow Tatcha. She believed in the blotting papers as a product, and she believed in the story behind it. She did what anyone would do when strapped for resources: she looked for free information and free inspiration. She went to her public library and wrote down the names of magazine editors and makeup artists she admired, and she started sending them blotting papers as PR packages. This personal touch and the story she told about the product allowed Tatcha to begin gaining traction. *Today*, *Vogue*, and *O, The Oprah Magazine* picked up the story, and Vicky started getting recognition.

During this time, she also sought out retailers but, unfortunately, was not successful. She heard time and time again that Tatcha wouldn't work and that no one was interested in Asian beauty. Companies like Shiseido, SK-II, and Shu Uemura had not yet found success in the US market, which did not bode well for commercializing Tatcha.

I was very surprised to hear that East Asian beauty ideals were not aspirational at this time, particularly because that contrasts with the popularity of East Asian products today. This popularity is particularly prevalent through the surge of K-beauty.

According to *The Business of Fashion*, the emergence of Asian beauty in America can be closely tied to the emergence of its most popular category, K-beauty. K-beauty, or Korean beauty, started gaining popularity in America in the mid-2010s, particularly with the emergence of gel creams and sheet masks. This growing demand in America was the result of a business strategy backed by the South Korean government. *The Cut* writes about how the Korean government, recognizing the lucrative potential of K-beauty exports, particularly paired with the international growth of Korean entertainment, K-pop and K-drama, developed several initiatives to help expand K-beauty internationally. Some of these initiatives included tax breaks for export-only businesses, supporting legal fees for companies to protect their brands overseas, but also personal support from former Korean President Park Geun-hye. This push for K-beauty, however, came in 2015, well after Vicky's first attempts at commercializing Tatcha.

Path to Success

Despite some positive press, Tatcha didn't immediately become the booming success it is now. Vicky had some steady revenue, but not enough to scale the business in a massive way. She even had a few offers for financial partnerships, but she was laser-focused on preserving the integrity and the story of her product (NPR). She described on *Behind Her Empire* that she continued to work, doing part-time consulting jobs while being a mom and spending seventy hours per week on Tatcha. The modest salary she did make she described as "lower than the lowest salary."

Vicky ran out of her initial batch of blotting paper and knew she wanted to capitalize on Tatcha's modest success by furthering the company's product line. However, she also knew she needed to find a reliable manufacturer to replicate the historical success of the Japanese products she had explored during her trip. To accomplish this, Vicky went back to Japan and found a lab in Tokyo where leading scientists took green tea, seaweed, and algae and combined them into formulas dictated by ancient Japanese techniques from the early 1800s. These became the products that healed Vicky's skin and became staples in her soon-to-be fully formed skin care line (Behind Her Empire).

In 2011, the vast majority of skin care brands were using ready-to-make formulas that someone with capital could personalize just slightly enough to brand the product as their own and bring it to market. There wasn't a big demand for clean products, and the e-commerce space was relatively new. The scientists in Tokyo that Vicky encountered recognized this homogenous market and understood her vision of reproducing ancient techniques to differentiate Tatcha from the competition.

This manufacturing technique was not cheap, and Vicky had to ask her friends and family for additional capital. She was lucky and was able to raise $1 million. Between the materials and the cost of working with manufacturers in Japan, she quickly burned through the funds and was forced to operate Tatcha out of her parents' garage in San Francisco.

I wish I could say that Tatcha really took off after what seemed like Vicky's second bout with bankruptcy. She had a lot of social capital and a lot of exposure after what she refers to as "the holy grail of press," which included a spread in *Vogue* and another appearance on *Today*. Unfortunately, this press only amounted to a single sale of a serum and continued rejections from retailers she wanted to partner with. As compelling as her story was, retailers still did not understand the appeal of Asian beauty.

Telling Her Story

The magic formula missing in Vicky's process thus far was an opportunity to tell the story of Tatcha herself. The press she got from products she'd previously shared with influencers included anecdotes about the quality of the items, which were great. However, what really sold Tatcha to a wider consumer base was the chance to tell her story on QVC in 2013. QVC, the television channel dedicated solely to home shopping, allowed Vicky to come in and speak to her consumers directly.

This is where Vicky's voice worked, and she was able to finally tell her story that helped her sell products. The solace she found in the ritualistic beauty in Japan and the struggles she faced to be able to share this treasure trove with others resonated with QVC viewers. Soon, the boxes of blotting paper that once took over the San Francisco garage grew into proper packaging for a wide range of products. After Vicky's successful showmanship on QVC, her entire inventory of products sold in eight minutes.

Financially stable after eight years, Vicky was finally seeing Tatcha succeed as the company gained fame and recognition and began to grow. Tatcha gave her success and recognition and furthered inclusion in the world of beauty and, most importantly, "the ability to recognize the beauty and power of the Asian heritage [she] had struggled to see in [her] youth" (Inc.). After the QVC appearance, Vicky's company began to turn a profit. Eventually, after she had ensured her brand was stable, she struck a minority deal with a private equity firm to support Tatcha's growing capital expenditures.

Tatcha Today

Vicky's questions when she started Tatcha were twofold: "Can I create something that's based on truth, that makes our clients feel genuinely cared for instead of diminished as women and as people?" and "Can I use the profits we generate and put that back into something that matters?" (Behind Her Empire).

Based on her success and the values of the company, the answer to these questions is a resounding yes. First, Vicky has seen the value of telling an authentic story based on truth. The story she was able to tell on QVC launched Tatcha to success. It is no secret, to this day, that aside from the quality of the products, Vicky told *POPSUGAR* that Tatcha's number one job is to "authentically share what we love and celebrate about Japanese culture." In a comment about healthy cultural exchange versus appropriation, Vicky talked about the fact that, yes, she is acutely aware and sensitive to the fact that she is not Japanese. The way she has decided to honor the heritage of her products is by making all products in Japan, sourcing all raw materials from Japan, having her products made by Japanese scientists, and ensure that her head of culture, Nami Onodera, is present at every conversation within the company.

To the question of putting the profits back into something that matters, since reaching financial stability (and arguably even before), giving back to the community has been a key driver of Tatcha's mission. According to the organization's website, in January 2014, when Tatcha's revenues had grown to $12 million, Vicky launched a one-to-one model where, for every full-sized product purchased, the company would fund one full day of school for Room to Read's Girl's Education Program (Room to Read).

This type of authentic story is what values-based buyers look for. How Japanese is your company, really, if you are producing products elsewhere and simply using geisha rituals to tell a good story? Credit goes where credit is due for Vicky because the type of probing that exists today did not exist in 2011 when Tatcha was born. These mechanisms to preserve a Japanese voice in her products did not come from a reaction to cancel culture; it came from a genuine desire to share the story of Japan.

Vicky named her company Tatcha, often accidentally yet appropriately tied to *tatehana*—a Japanese flower-arranging technique known to show the beauty found in simplicity. The name Tatcha came around in a time when Vicky was blindly searching for meaning and just wanted to create a product that sounds and feels "like an exhale, like a breath of fresh air." *Tatcha*. Did you say it out loud yet?

NANCY TWINE'S BRIOGEO

———

I can't say firsthand what a career in finance does to you, but it's become clear through my research for this book that it clearly breeds disillusionment in finance and genius in the beauty industry. Nancy Twine has had a career path similar to some of the other women in this book, and she's only worked at two places her whole life. After starting her tenure in finance at Goldman Sachs, she started her very own natural hair care company, Briogeo.

I started using Briogeo at the recommendation of a business school classmate, and every time I use it, I say Briogeo in a posh French accent because that's how I feel when I use fancy hair products. My classmate and I both have textured, damaged hair, and while we have both perfected the twenty-minute hair straightening routine over decades, it has completely fried and damaged our hair. We have both been on clean hair care journeys to nourish our hair and help support the texture it naturally takes, rather than frying it on a daily basis and trying to pass that off as natural. I've tried everything, from concocting my own uneven avocado-honey-egg-based hair mixture or washing my hair with nothing but apple cider vinegar and baking soda, all without being able to find or afford natural hair products.

Briogeo is expensive. It's not a product everyone can afford, and even though I have a large tub of one of its deep conditioning products, I ritualistically use as little as possible, trying to save it for as long as it will last. It's a product I've put on birthday and Christmas wish lists so I can have someone else foot my hair care bill for once. At the same time, calling Briogeo fancy is ironic because the product started from the simplicity of Nancy watching her grandmother create these products at home.

Nancy's Childhood

Much like some of the other profiles we've seen in this book, Nancy's relationship with beauty and self-care began in her childhood. Her grandmother's kitchen was filled with natural ingredients to create the beauty products that ended up becoming the core concept for her hair care brand. In an interview with *Makeup*, Nancy recalls struggling with her hair when she was younger "because the products on the market were just not right for [her] hair texture." Using natural products was a tradition in her family as Nancy spent time with her mother "concocting and mixing [their] own beauty products and treatments from scratch."

Although I am not equipped to speak to this through personal experiences, it is no secret that hair is a key part of the experiences of Black women in America. Princess Jones, in *The Mash-Up Americans*, writes that the Black hair industry is valued at $774 million "because we are serious about our hair. Our hair can affect our moods. Our hair has its own vocabulary. It bonds us together in the style successes and struggles." Mamona writes that Black hair has been an "integral feature of Black history." It has served as a way to identify family background, tribe, and social status in African civilizations; symbolic statements of pride and inclusion during Civil Rights movements; as well as an "ode to creativity" for Black women.

While a source of celebration and inclusion, Black hair has also been discriminated against. Examples of this discrimination range from deeming Black hairstyles "unprofessional" in the workplace to, as NBC reports, keeping Black beauty products under lock and key in stores. More generally, though, there has also been a lack of products, lack of representation in product development, and lack of attention on Black hair care products at the industry level.

Nancy's mother was a chemist and a physician, she explained during an interview with her alma mater, the University of Virginia. Her skills as a scientist allowed her to understand, break down, and share with Nancy the intricate mix of ingredients behind her family's history with hair care. Nancy recalls looking at her mother's success as a scientist while reflecting on her own journey as an entrepreneur, that "from such a young age, being able to see a black woman really thrive and grow a practice... I just internally really saw that as a theme for my life, which is you can do anything and being a female or being a minority doesn't stop you from pursuing your dreams" (Makeup).

The entrepreneurial spirit flowed from her mother and followed Nancy throughout her whole life. As early as high school, Nancy was indoctrinated into the world of turning her passions into a business through making jewelry and other crafts that she would sell to her classmates (UVA). She was thrilled to earn money doing what she loved. As a result, according to the aptly named podcast *Second Life*, she sought out the best way to supplement her at-home education and decided to get an undergraduate degree in business.

Nancy then did what most undergraduate finance majors do: looked for on-campus recruiting events and landed herself a role at Goldman Sachs. Her first job in commodity sales and trading helped her monitor and understand pricing fluctuations in raw materials, which ended up becoming a key contributor to her tactics for Briogeo's product procurement. Nancy's career evolved at Goldman Sachs over seven years, ultimately leading to her role as the commodities sales and trading vice president. While her time there was a significant learning experience where she built strong networks, learned how to prioritize clients, and worked in teams to accomplish larger goals, she knew it wasn't her future and started to explore next steps.

Nancy's final wake-up call was, unfortunately, losing her mother suddenly in a tragic car accident (UVA). It was the first time she had lost someone so close to her, an unfortunate situation that forced her to consider that "we all owe it to ourselves to discover what we're most passionate about."

What was the path she was passionate about? She'd been at Goldman Sachs for seven years and had worked her way up to a vice president role. She didn't know what it was like to work anywhere else, and there she was, having left a job where she had moved up the rungs of the ladder. She recalled from her childhood that her best memories were recreating what her mother and grandmother, and maybe even generations before them, had perfected over time. For Nancy, passion came through these moments, so that's what she decided to work on.

Briogeo and the Beauty Industry

Nancy began spending her nights and weekends researching the beauty business at New York City's small business library, according to *Forbes*. Overlapping a bit with her time at Goldman Sachs, Nancy spent the final years of her tenure as a financial executive searching for a lab and a chemist to create nontoxic products for textured hair.

She knew she wanted to create a "clean, natural brand that offered solutions for every hair type, texture, need, ethnicity, background, and person" (Makeup). Her desire and background helpfully coincided with the growing consumer demand for clean products in the early 2010s. The growth of retailers, as described by *Allure*, like Whole Foods and products like Burt's Bees, increased interest in natural products, while mediums like Gwyneth Paltrow's *Goop* and clean beauty pop-up stores in California in the late 2000s became platforms where natural beauty options became popularized.

These days, demand for chemical transparency is even being backed by Congress through initiatives like the Personal Care Products Safety Act introduced by Senator Dianne Feinstein of California in 2017. The bill has not gained traction since, but it's an interesting and not often seen step toward regulating ingredients in personal care products beyond the FDA's loose framework for beauty and cosmetics today.

In the midst of a growing demand for natural products and changing attitudes toward beauty, Nancy, in 2013, used her savings to find a lab that would commercialize and recreate the formulas she knew from her childhood. She would eventually launch her natural hair care line under the name Briogeo, as described by their website—Brio, an Italian word meaning "full of life, vivid, and unique," and Geo, a Latin word meaning "of Earth or nature."

Inclusion was also a core part of Nancy's brand conception. Of course, she wanted to help others navigate experiences of having trouble with hair care. When she went shopping for hair care products, she found that the product offerings were always very segregated and found herself having to go to a different corner of the drugstore to find "multicultural" hair care products (*Forbes*). This is something I *still* see in drugstores and superstores today; the Black-owned, "diverse" brands are always in a small corner of the store, and sometimes they are on locked shelves.

This issue of locking up Black hair products became significantly more publicized following the murder of George Floyd in summer 2020, as reported by *US News*. Despite drugstore chains like CVS and Walgreens also participating in this discriminatory act, Walmart became the center of attention for this heinous behavior after a federal discrimination lawsuit filed in 2018. Apparently, Walmart was interested in protecting its products and cited shoplifting as a concern, but none of the products for the general population were ever on locked shelves. Two years later, amid protests across the nation focused on discriminatory behavior by largely white institutions, Walmart said it would ban the practice. How nice of them to finally comply after years of continuing this behavior, even after getting sued! For this and many other reasons, Nancy made it Briogeo's mission to target customers by hair texture and developed her product line in that way. Customers would be identified "by hair texture (wavy, coily, dry, thin) rather than by ethnicity" (*Forbes*).

Investing in Briogeo

Nancy worked on Briogeo every free second she had and self-financed the company for over six years. During this time, she continued to pitch to investors who were largely "involved in the tech industry and [lacking] knowledge of the beauty industry," she said to Talk Route. It was a discouraging experience to continue pitching to white men in tech who would ask, "Wait, this is a shampoo, right?" she said to *NPR*. Even lightly browsing the venture capital articles from around this time in 2012, one on CB Insights, for example, they all seemed to focus on Menlo Park, medical devices, mobile customer relationship management platforms, and other things "techy." Imagine being a Black woman pitching an inclusive, natural hair care brand to this crowd. I can't help but think of other Briogeos that were passed on during this time because of the lack of diversity in venture capitalism, fueled by a growing tech bubble. How many more Briogeos could we have had by now?

Eventually, Nancy was able to find Philip Palmedo, who agreed on investing based on his belief in the product but still considered Briogeo a risk (*Forbes*). "Believing in the person" was important to Philip, so he invested $150,000 in 2013, which not only gave Nancy a seed investment for product development but also external validation for the product (Talk Route).

Finally able to shop the product around without worrying about the financial burden of dipping into her personal savings, Nancy secured Urban Outfitters and Fred Segal, a trendy LA boutique, as Briogeo's first retail buyers. To supplement the retail route, Nancy also attended a trade show in 2013, CosmoProf in Las Vegas, where she met buyers from

Sephora and secured an agreement in 2014 for them to feature Briogeo products on their US and Canada websites. With Sephora's growing focus on expanding its hair care market and the still-growing customer demand for natural products, Briogeo made it to the shelves, making Nancy Twine the youngest Black woman to have a product in Sephora.

Soon after the deal with Sephora was struck, Nancy gave notice at Goldman Sachs and dedicated her efforts to growing the brand full time (NPR). VMG notes that Briogeo continued to flourish under her leadership as she developed innovative and category-creating products like the Scalp Revival line, making Briogeo one of the early pioneers of scalp care products. Recognizing Nancy's success, VMG partners decided to invest in the company, and Nancy agreed, noting that she needed capital for the company that was scaling very quickly and coming up with new and improved challenges to go along with the growth. Briogeo has been profitable *every* year since its existence and, despite an economic recession, was expected to make $40 million in sales as of 2020 (NPR).

Briogeo Today

Nancy's experiences as a Black female entrepreneur have grown her interest in paving the way for others like her. Being able to launch and support a product through success comes with a lot of privilege and is not at all an accessible process. Nancy's story shows the variety of privileges needed to enter the beauty industry—personal capital for initial expenditures, a unicorn investor who is interested in the story behind a product as much as the product itself, wit and business background to be able to recognize and address a growing demand, and a well-loved recipe passed down through generations in your family.

Today, Briogeo has become one of the first companies to "successfully blur the lines and have a truly diverse client base" without relying on a "multicultural" label to reach different customers (UVA). The elephant in the room, though, is that Briogeo is an expensive product—not a celebrity-level, high-end hair care product, but the shampoo and conditioner combo, for example, costs about ten times as much as the average shampoo and conditioner at a Walmart would. Despite a higher price point, Nancy has "taken the time to do her homework" and has produced a product that is not only high-end and nontoxic but is priced slightly below other premium hair brands, allowing her to successfully tap into the almost $500 million worth of hair products purchased by Black customers annually (*Forbes*).

Even so, her products are expensive, and aside from Toni Ko's NYX Cosmetics and Amanda Johnson and KJ Miller's Mented, I'd argue that most of the products discussed in this book are on the more expensive side of things. Pieces like "Why Organic Products Are More Expensive" highlight how high-end products often come with high costs. It is because they have shorter shelf-lives and more expensive raw materials that are pricier to source, and often, more sustainable manufacturing that also comes with a higher cost. I do worry that natural products that are meant to be accessible to an ethnically diverse client base will be completely inaccessible to a large majority of that population.

Still, Nancy has found commercial success blurring the lines of what it means to be an "ethnic" product and having products for Black women on the shelves of major retailers rather than in a locked corner of a dingy CVS. Her company is growing; soon it'll be a globally available product. With companies like Briogeo making a mark on caring for and representing diverse hair types, maybe we are one step closer to fundamentally changing the way we see, interpret, and treat people with different hair. Who knows?

HEELA YANG AND CAMILA PIEROTTI'S SOL DE JANEIRO

I was gifted a set of Sol de Janeiro products for Christmas. Much like my Briogeo products, I use them sparingly, trying to save them for as long as they will last. I text my friend every time I use it to let her know that although the Coco Cabana Cream looks and smells like delicious yogurt, so far, I have successfully resisted the urge to eat it.

Sol de Janeiro is exactly like it sounds—it's warm, looks splashy, smells incredible, and makes you feel good about your skin. The bright yellows and blues and the sunny graphics that adorn the packaging always make me wish that I was on a beach somewhere. Co-founder Heela Yang described her experiences in Brazil on a Sol de Janeiro YouTube video: "On the beach you see people, women, men of all shapes, all sizes, all colors, just having so much fun. ... They're playing with their skin, their hair, they're putting stuff in their hair and then letting the sun soak in and jumping into the water, coming back out putting more of something else in. It's an amazing festival on the beach."

Sol de Janeiro's founding team can be described as a geographic intersection. It's comprised of Heela, a Korean American from New York who moved to Brazil when she got married to a Japanese American Brazilian man; Camila Pierotti, originally from Brazil and later moved to New York; and Marc Capra, a New Yorker who moved to Brazil after a single visit to the beaches.

Sol de Janeiro is a newer company. It was started in 2016 by this group of three who share a passion for the seductive Brazilian beauty culture. Heela said on *Get The Gloss* that her Brazilian beach experience is "inclusivity with a twist of playfulness." Both she and Camila are enamored and captivated by people of all shapes and colors being ritualistic with their skin care, like the skin-enhancing routines on the beaches of Brazil. That is exactly what they wanted to bring to the States.

Camila Pierotti

Camila, as a native of Brazil herself, also had a fun and playful experience growing up on the beaches of Rio de Janeiro. She described her childhood as being part of a "warm, Latin, affectionate culture where everyone is wearing fewer clothes but also very affectionate toward each other." She's "personally not obsessed with beauty" but sees this inherent act of taking care of yourself and taking care of your skin as a core part of her personal beauty routine. "It's not about what cream I'm going to use," she said, "but it's about taking five to ten minutes to smooth my feet or to moisturize my skin." This practice of taking care of your skin and your body is part of a Brazilian's getting ready process, and Camila is no stranger to it.

Camila moved to the United States and got her undergraduate degree from Georgetown University in 2001. In *Skincare*'s "Career Diaries," she described how her career began in the beauty world, where she worked in marketing at major companies like Clinique and NARS Cosmetics. During her tenure in beauty marketing, she learned the fundamentals of the business, the "best practices for executing programs," and "how to maneuver through a less structured environment." These skills were all necessary in launching and navigating products in the world of beauty.

Heela Yang

Originally from Seoul, Heela also moved to the United States at a young age. She went to Harvard for college, Yale for a master's in East Asian studies, and then worked in her father's political campaign in the Korean National Assembly. This career path turned out to be challenging and unenjoyable for Heela, so she left the political sector and began her tenure in finance through a role at Goldman Sachs, after which she landed a spot at Harvard Business School.

Heela's corporate career in beauty began after business school, particularly cultivated by her role as director of global skincare strategy and director of marketing at Clinique Laboratories. Heela was attracted to this industry "because it's dynamic, competitive, and it combines both left and right brains" (Get The Gloss).

Heela's relationship with beauty, according to *Women's Wear Daily*, is a bit more focused on her background as a

Korean American and her exposure to K-beauty products through her family. When she eventually moved to Brazil, she saw that the focus on beauty was not just on skin care but enhanced by attitude and confidence in taking care of the whole body. Seeing this focus on body skin care in Brazil juxtaposed with what she was used to seeing on the shelves of New York, Heela couldn't help but notice a missing piece of the market. Body care in America had only been focused on body wash and body lotion through drugstore brands (think Aveeno) and nothing else on the high-end shelves.

Beginning of Sol

Camila and Heela met in 2003, when they were both working in the beauty industry. I heard from their PR team that "Camila's desk was directly outside of Heelas' office, and the two instantly hit it off!" They bonded over their interest in the beauty industry and their mutual love for Brazil, but they lost touch after Heela moved to Brazil and Camila moved to another team. Thankfully, they were able to reconnect five years later when Heela moved back to New York, and shortly after, Sol de Janeiro was born.

Sol de Janeiro started in 2015, launching with three products that focused on unexpected parts of the body: butt, feet, and body hair (WWD). Selling products that were so specific did not start out as an easy process. Heela and Camila were essentially creating a new category of higher-end body products, *and* they were selling for specific body parts that people did not typically consider in the self-care or skin care category.

Outside of the products being specific, there were other nuances to Sol de Janeiro's initial offerings that broke a lot of rules in the beauty business. First, the products are very colorful—and what might yellow and blue packaging on body lotion remind you of? Sunscreen. Heela and Camila were initially warned that the product's color would be associated with sunscreen and that it would unnecessarily pigeonhole the products into a summer category (Breaking Beauty). Second, they were told not to put Bum Bum in a product name. It was a strange thing to do, and there was no knowing how customers would react to a product that is specifically made for butt-firming.

Thankfully, they didn't listen. They stayed true to the fun and playful message they wanted to promote through their products. They wanted to bring Brazil's sunshine to the dark streets of New York through the bright packaging and were adamant about keeping the vision they had alive. Luckily, the uniqueness of the brand is what ended up getting them a meeting with Sephora.

Around this time in 2015, Yahoo describes that consumers were looking for products that were focused on "effortless beauty." In fact, Sol de Janeiro can be considered an early entrant into the natural beauty movement that has been rampant over the past few years. Given this demand, when the founders met with Sephora, they were extremely interested in the revenue potential of such a unique product. They were so interested that Sephora sent over a contract on the same day to stock their shelves with Sol de Janeiro immediately (The Glossy Beauty). Today, the Brazilian Bum Bum Cream is one of the highest-selling products at Sephora and is universally beloved by so many consumers that it has a cultlike following (Breaking Beauty).

One of the reasons for this commercial success was also that the product looks, feels, and smells so incredibly good—so good that you can't help but to want to eat a dollop of the lotion with a large spoon. "You smell good" is apparently a well-loved compliment in Brazil. "Going back to that hot, humid climate and affectionate culture," said Camila, "you're in weather that is prone to make you sweat," so, she said, "you smell good" is one of the best compliments you can get.

The perfumery of the products was anything but a happy accident. The team wanted to create a scent that would induce a mouth-watering reaction, and so they did. The fragrance needed to be "delicious and irresistible, but unlike any other scent on the market." Eventually, the initial products landed on a scrumptious blend of pistachio and salted caramel (Yahoo).

Sol de Janeiro Today

Heela and Camila both relished in breaking away from the repetitive products and starting off a little differently in the entrepreneurial world of beauty, and that is exactly what Sol de Janeiro is known for. The company, both small and nimble, continued to find success in being creative and innovative, which became "very possible and much easier to do than when working within large, established companies" (Get The Gloss). Being a smaller company allowed Sol de Janeiro to quickly react to customer demand. This meant that they could create a line of fragrance products based on their known and loved mouth-watering scents (WWD).

COVID-19 brought another opportunity—necessity, really—for a company like Sol de Janeiro to restructure its strategy and focus aggressively on the customers' asks (The Glossy Beauty). According to McKinsey, the global beauty industry has been impacted significantly by the pandemic, mainly through decreased purchases and increased e-commerce activities, which are not always enough to offset losses. It has become more important than ever to identify customer needs exactly and respond accordingly.

Sol de Janeiro's response to the pandemic has been to keep working, keep the staff employed, and really reconnect with customers to understand why they are buying Sol de Janeiro's products (The Glossy Beauty). Customers are interested in continuing The Lipstick Effect—buying cheap but high-impact cosmetics despite economic downturns. By continuing to bring small pieces of luxury through its fragrance line, Sol de Janeiro was able to provide its main consumer base a much-needed consistency. The team was able to pivot so quickly that they even started to make hand sanitizers with their signature scents, and I've seen their product line grow ever since.

So what can we say about the future of Sol de Janeiro? In 2019, the brand received $14.5 million in funding from Prelude Growth Partners, a firm that invests in clean skin care, organic juice, and other health and wellness products. The quick pivot to developing products consumers needed, fragrances and hand sanitizers, afforded them the unique luxury, even during the pandemic, to sell 900 percent more than the second-best-selling fragrance (The Glossy Beauty). Through their products, they've managed to create "a safe haven, for comfort and feeling well" and a much-needed teleportation to a Rio de Janeiro beach.

The story they wanted to tell through the packaging, scents, product development, description, and even intention has stayed tried and true. The whimsy that Heela and Camila created has so far been protected and grown by their strategy to keep messaging functions like marketing in-house to better control and stay consistent with their authentic story (Breaking Beauty).

Heela and Camila's insights and hope for the future of beauty are very aligned with what we see in this book. Heela is excited for the "smaller, nimble, and niche brand builders that are socially and digitally progressive" to be able to finally see the light of day (Get the Gloss). In an industry primarily driven by conglomerates, Heela says, "knowing that niche players can make a meaningful difference gives me hope and motivation." Camila, too, wants to see more of an intention for beauty to be "about taking the time for yourself and taking care of yourself." When we talked about beauty and beach culture, she said to me, "If you want to go to the beach and it becomes a huge production every time, you're not going to enjoy yourself at the beach." She wants Sol de Janeiro to be the only accessory you need to feel confident at the beach.

More tactically, though, Camila believes in the power of knowing your brand and being able to tell that story. As businesses grow, the brand will evolve and have a different life. "It's extremely scary and also exhilarating, so use those feelings to propel you forward," she advised. At the same time, recognizing the success of her company's message to flaunt what you have, her advice is to "have your team truly understand the ethos" and follow the company values consistently.

Beauty in Brazil

As I close out this chapter, something continues to gnaw at me. Heela and Camila are both champions of body diversity, and their devotion to the cause is clear from Sol de Janeiro's Instagram account. One quick look at the home page and you will be instantly greeted not only with the brand's signature yellow and blue but with a full spectrum of different bodies of different colors.

However, I was quite surprised to read about the body-inclusive culture of Brazil's beaches, and even after reading the descriptions shared by Heela and Camila, I was still quite skeptical. Both slender, light-skinned women, I can't help but dig into the shared feeling of inclusion in the beach culture described by our founders above. In the United States, going to the beach has been a not-so-fun experience for many women who do not fit the "ideal" body standards set by society. I wanted to validate their statements through a more diverse lens: Is it true that Brazilian beaches are truly a worry-free zone for everyone?

Heela's first time on the beaches of Rio, for example, sounds like an experience that would have been jarring if it were anywhere but in Brazil. While getting ready for the beach, a friend suggested that it's okay to wear a two-piece bikini while she was pregnant (Breaking Beauty). Uncomfortable at first, Heela decided to wear her bikini. Once she got to the beach, however, she saw that no one noticed. No one cared; no one was looking at her. Instead, she saw a very diverse array of bodies simply enjoying the beach.

I was surprised by Heela's account because it seems as though Brazilian beauty standards and American beauty standards are limited in similar ways. *Jetset Magazine* reported that "Brazilian media outlets and advertisements on television promote a Western aesthetic and feed consumers an oversexualized image for women to follow." Neidyn Regalado, a Latina makeup artist based in the United States, shared her all-too-familiar experience of beauty standards creating a barrier for her. She said, "It's almost like I feel like it's my fault that I sometimes don't have a color that will match a woman of color. Even with myself, I find it hard to find a concealer that matches my own skin tone."

The color-matching struggles have already been highlighted in this book, so what I'm interested in exploring is body beauty standards in Brazil and how inclusive they really are. Camila described the beach culture as being "not any sort of universal standard to achieve; it's a feeling—feeling comfortable and happy in your own skin" (The Glossy Beauty).

I read Bianca Costa Sales' heartbreaking, eye-opening, soul-crushing piece in *Adamah Media,* published in February 2020. In it, she talks about the personal cost of catering to Brazilian beauty standards set forth by the likes of Gisele Bündchen. She states that Brazil has the second-most cosmetic procedures and plastic surgeries in the world, feeding into a "strange sense of pride and achievement in being able to finally fix the bodily imperfections that clearly have been so bothersome."

Bianca then cites Brazil's complex and impactful colonial history as contributing to not only the ethnic diversity seen in the country today but also in the racist beauty ideals that come with it. For example, "an everyday reflection of beauty's discriminatory bias in Brazil is the fact that people usually refer to curly hair as 'bad hair' without giving a second thought to how racist it is that straight hair is automatically considered 'good hair.'" Does that sound familiar to anyone?

Related to beach culture, though, there was a movement in 2017 called "Day of Fat People on the Beach," where fifty fat people went to the beach for fun, sun, and discussions on fatphobia. The article on *Vice* featuring this movement also describes the experiences of fat people going to the beaches of Rio, as well as their struggles to find a swimsuit because of the lack of inclusive sizing at stores.

This is not to take away from Sol de Janeiro's mission, which is still meant to be about inclusivity in the company ethos and inclusivity in how it communicates this ethos. This is, however, meant to question and shed light on the beauty standards that the brand actively fights against. Westernized standards of beauty are universally pervasive, and Sol de Janeiro is just one of many companies interested in changing these standards.

"No rules. Just BODY JOY," says their page on Instagram, alongside photos of all kinds of women who so look joyful on the sand, it just might get me to go to the beach.

DEEPICA MUTYALA'S LIVE TINTED

It's January 2018, and Deepica Mutyala shares a YouTube series, Living Tinted, to document the launch of her company. She examines a table and floor in her living room covered in headshots. There are photos strewn about, piled on top of each other, made up of darker-skinned South Asian faces, light-skinned faces, and medium tones—the whole spectrum. These are photos of potential women that will serve as the guiding principle for the customer base of her brand, aptly named Live Tinted. She looks at all these photos and wonders why no one is smiling. "Why so serious, girl?" she says to one of them.

Deepica grew up in Houston, Texas, and her experience "surrounded by blonde hair and blue eyes" and Eurocentric beauty standards stood in stark contrast with her own look as a dark-skinned South Indian woman. Over time, she went through the identity crisis that many multicultural kids, myself included, have felt after "not seeing [herself] represented anywhere, especially in the media and absolutely not in the beauty industry." Eventually, she decided to create her own environment where people like her could feel comfortable embracing their culture through her brand, Live Tinted.

The Beginning of Tinted

Picture Deepica, a "little brown girl whose mom would put red lipstick on [her]" during her classical dance recitals. She now finds it ironic that she ended up creating her all-in-one hue sticks for Live Tinted because her mom would use that red lipstick during her recitals as a blush and eyeshadow combo.

Deepica's goal from a young age was to get involved in the beauty industry and learn to grow and share her love for makeup. In fact, Deepica's and my experiences as young women experimenting with makeup are eerily similar. She talked about how she "would wear foundation and powders that were lighter" than her own skin tone. She also mentioned looking at Maybelline products in the drug stores and not finding products for herself that were in her price range but later being able to shop at Sephora, which was a big accomplishment for us both. "College was when I went to the department stores and MACs of the world," she described. "After that was the Sephora life, like, that to me was a luxury." This was the case for me too—using the too-light, limited skin tones offered by cheaper brands while really wanting to get my hands on the expensive stuff.

Despite wanting to work in the world of beauty, as a first-generation American, Deepica decided to go a "safer" route and get a degree in marketing from The University of Texas at Austin. Still, she wanted to be beauty-adjacent, so, as she said on Jay Shetty's podcast, she would enter this industry first from the corporate side of things, hoping later on to be able to work directly with the products.

After completing her degree, Deepica landed a job as an inventory deployment analyst for Limited Brands, supporting Victoria's Secret PINK. Here, she was able to build her knowledge of the beauty industry through her work. She first interned at L'Oréal, then worked through brand management at Birchbox, and eventually explored and embraced makeup through her side hustle, her YouTube channel.

The Viral Video

The video that catapulted Deepica into the makeup world was a surprisingly casual one. Only her second video on YouTube, the clip begins with Deepica, just out of bed and still in her pajamas, teaching her audience "How to Cover Dark Under Eye Circles." The idea is simple: if you have dark circles under your eyes, use bright orange/red lipstick to neutralize the dark discoloration before putting on concealer. It's funny—I think I watched this video a few years ago because it happened to come up on my feed somehow. I didn't know back then that I'd be writing this book, that I'd have a chance to interview Deepica, or that her brand would become a poster company for South Asian women.

Cost effective and immediately applicable (since most women have red lipstick lying around), this technique blew up on the internet. Over four million views later, her YouTube career was off to a booming success in 2015. As of 2021, the video has over ten million views.

Deepica has often described going viral on the internet as an "out-of-body experience" (Jay Shetty). Her YouTube career started as a casual way for her to share beauty tips with her friends and was the first step toward Live Tinted. After her video went viral, she was contacted by *Buzzfeed*, *Refinery29*, and *Today*. With this viral video in her back pocket, Deepica decided to take advantage of the situation and pursue the world of beauty full time.

Despite having a viral video, Deepica still had to find her footing in the digital world and work toward changing the representation of beauty in the industry. She was not a trained makeup artist, and while she tried to diversify her offerings beyond her viral video, she struggled to do so. In trying to develop new content for social media, she found YouTube itself to be a helpful outlet to share the challenges and career decisions she was facing. She was convinced that telling stories particularly focused on the challenges women of color face in the beauty world would be her "brand." Using this angle of sharing her struggles, she launched a separate digital platform, Tinted, in February 2018.

Tinted became an outlet for Deepica and an outlet for many other women whose skin tones did fall into "conventional" shades. It served as a community and a forum for these women to share their stories, and it eventually became the launchpad for her beauty product line, Live Tinted.

Product Launch

Deepica's online presence was growing steadily, but the world of beauty still did not properly represent people who looked like her. She sought to find a solution for people who look like us. Much of the content and vision for her company is deeply rooted in Deepica's intention to make the beauty industry more equitable and celebratory for women of all shades, dark- or light-skinned.

Financial shortcomings are a huge barrier to entry in this industry, commonly seen throughout the profiles in this book, and Live Tinted was not immune to this. Growing a business and dedicating time to Live Tinted were clear priorities for Deepica, and both were complicated by the financial realities of starting a beauty brand, she said on the podcast *I Suck At Life*. Knowing that the launch of this company would be impactful to her mission of inclusion, she decided to go for it. Still, she had to figure out how to spend her time living, eating, and breathing Live Tinted when she knew her income came from the time-consuming work she did as an influencer. "In my mind, I always wanted to be a boss—but being a boss is not just a quote on Instagram, it's a lot, lot more than that," Deepica realized as she grappled with this tension.

This is one of the more difficult parts of entering the beauty industry. Even in the indie beauty world, with new, niche brands emerging, it is incredibly expensive to start a product line. Even for someone like Deepica, who had a passion and background in beauty, it took the financial potential of a wildly viral video to nudge her into taking the plunge.

How much does it cost to start a beauty brand? It is highly dependent on your goals as the founder. In response to a 2019 *Beauty Independent* article asking whether $1.5 million is enough to start a beauty brand, Julianne Robicheau, founder of Robi Luxury Skin Care, says that "many beauty brands have launched with modest budgets and become successful, so I don't think $1.5 million is the magic number." However, she then goes on to say, "If the goal is to be the next big thing within the first year, then, yes, a $1 million budget might be needed."

The other responses to this question in the article are generally along similar lines of "No, $1.5 million is not necessary, unless you want to be successful in this industry, then you need $1.5 million." Well, everyone wants to be successful, and $1.5 million is not chump change. So how are women of color, who tend to be financially disenfranchised, supposed to contribute to the growth of this industry? Without easy and equitable access to this massive amount of capital needed, how can we make this industry more representative?

Inclusion in Living Tinted

Deepica's goal with Live Tinted is not for it to be a limited campaign for being inclusive or to limit her products specifically for brown women, but rather to build a "home to show a whole range of women, [a] whole range of skin tones." As Live Tinted grew, August 2019 marked an important financial milestone for her as Live Tinted raised an initial round of funds from investors like Bobbi Brown, Hayley Barna, Payal Kadakia, Andy Dunn, Jaime Schmidt, Shivani Siroya, and Shilpa Shah, all of whom have found success in the beauty industry, according to *BeautyMatter*.

When I spoke with Deepica, we mainly discussed inclusion, representation, and what she wants her brand to stand for. Before receiving a line of funding from her champions mentioned above, her initial conversations with other investors were not particularly lucrative because the focus of her products was on South Asian women. "They all said I was thinking too small," she recalled as she tried to grapple with the idea of "too small" to describe the entire South Asian market. She said, "Even if I just said South Asian people, two billion people were considered a small market scope."

The South Asian beauty industry is growing, and much like K-beauty, products like Anomaly (founded by Hollywood star Priyanka Chopra Jonas) and Kulfi Beauty (founded by Ipsy alum Priyanka Ganjoo) are "putting their heritage and rituals front and center as the craft emerging beauty brands, stories, and communities," writes *Glossy*. Kulfi, which means popsicle, has a product development strategy that solely focuses on the South Asian market. "Products are tested on South Asian consumers inspired by their needs and wants," along with Kulfi Bites, a supplemental content site focused on profiling members of this target market and creating a sense of community affiliated with the brand.

There are approximately five million South Asians in the United States. Even if a small portion of this population bought Live Tinted products, there is an opportunity to easily recoup the $1.5 million investment.

Deepica's goals have not wavered even as the company has grown to form more partnerships with influencers, develop more products, and even form alliances with other brands. Live Tinted recently collaborated with Beautyblender, and even through the collaborations, the brand continues to be a champion of elevating the voices of women who are revolutionizing representation in this industry.

Deepica's goal has been first and foremost for the brand to "normalize diversity and make it so representation and inclusivity is just a standard in this industry." She wants "this brand to stand for a greater purpose," and she will continue to push for this no matter the cost.

Future of Beauty

Deepica's concrete advice to hopeful entrepreneurs is to:

First, just go for it, keeping in mind the risk. She has been vocal about the fact that she didn't wait for her ten million views to happen. She used the tools at hand—her iPhone to shoot the video and a treasure trove of ideas—without making the excuse that she didn't have the fancy equipment to produce content.

She wasn't worried about what others would think or that no one would find her videos useful. She saw an opportunity to share a tip she'd been using for years and went for it. "You just have to start" is her main advice, and it's because she didn't overthink it. "Always find a way to do the step one without taking a huge risk," she said.

Second, think about starting off your product with a niche audience. "That's what I did with this color-correcting niche that hit ten million people." This eventually ended up becoming a key customer base for her business. This market is cluttered; it's oversaturated, "but if you think about what you can uniquely own and position your brand around," trust that instinct and start testing those theories.

Deepica's story resonated with me so much. Perhaps it is because we share similar backgrounds and have a history of not quite fitting in. Houston and New York City (where I grew up) have different levels of representation of people who look like us. Deepica's experience of living in a sea of blonde hair and blue eyes were different from my childhood, but I think we can both relate to the feeling of being an outsider. With Live Tinted, I can shop around the store and buy anything I want, knowing that someone developing this product has thought about how someone like me would look wearing it.

It is not fun to grow up different. It is especially not fun to know you are different, go to the store to pick out a product, then be reminded that you are, in fact, so different that there isn't anything for you to buy. I hope the work that Deepica and many others in this book are doing inch us closer and closer to erasing that feeling completely.

AMANDA JOHNSON AND KJ MILLER'S MENTED COSMETICS

———

Allegedly over a bottle of wine (when most great ideas are born), Kristen Jones (KJ) Miller and Amanda Johnson thought about the very Eurocentric "nude" lipstick product and decided to do something to address the color exclusivity of nude products. Their product testing method was simple— Does it show up on my skin? As they sought to create (pig) Mented products specifically for women of color, as written by the National Retail Foundation, they wanted to make a set of nude lipsticks that was appropriate for the women who were not able to find a fitting product in the market.

If you are at all darker than the color of mayonnaise, you know this problem all too well. Skin-color tights not looking like skin, bandages showing up way too light, nude lipsticks making us look like we got a skin graft on our lips. This is exactly a part of the discrepancy Amanda and KJ wanted to address—to bring nude lipsticks that are fit for and look good on people of color.

Amanda Johnson

Amanda's experience with nude-shaded products began at a young age with her training as a classical ballet dancer, she said on NBC. The brutal and challenging art form, arguably already an exclusive space, made her feel even more out of place with the very pink tights that ballet dancers wear. Amanda couldn't find one to fit her skin tone, so she had to recolor the tights on her own for her performances. She said, "I remember my mom on the weekends before big performances having to dye my tights in the kitchen sink in tea so that they could become nude."

As Amanda started experimenting with makeup, she had the experience many of us have had: walking into a store and not finding any product made for us, or even seeing women who looked like us in ad campaigns. I've already talked specifically about the lack of color representation in foundations, concealers, and other face makeup products. There are, however, also instances of color cosmetics that do not work for women of color: pastel eyeshadows, for example, that are not pigmented well enough to show up on darker skin even after three to four applications. "Nude" lip colors, which became very popular in 2017-18, share the same issue.

Eventually, Amanda made her way to Howard University and got her degree in, you guessed it, finance, before moving over to her first job at, you guessed it, Goldman Sachs. She worked at Goldman for over two years and moved over to a marketing role before starting her MBA at Harvard Business School, where she met her co-founder, KJ Miller.

KJ Miller

KJ's story with makeup begins much later. She said to *Glossy* that she never really wore lipstick, but she understood Black women's financial influence on beauty. When she was growing up, diversity and inclusion efforts were a "trendy" part of social media, and these efforts weren't necessarily focused on making foundational changes. Diversity in beauty for KJ has historically fluctuated: "It depends on what models are on the runway, what's chic in a season," even though "the reality is that people of color have always been around."

KJ went to Harvard for her undergraduate degree and finished with a degree in philosophy. She shared with *Refinery29* that she ended up landing a job at Kmart's corporate offices and was essentially hired to course correct for this struggling department store. During her time, she saw that the buyers at Kmart were really the ones driving the decision-making. In order to have a say, she decided to get a job that would get her a seat at the table, even though it meant she would need to take a demotion to an assistant buyer position.

At this job, KJ knew she wanted to put an emphasis on the learning experience over a flashy title or a flashy brand name. She wanted to be a big fish in a small pond rather than stay with the multibillion-dollar company she was previously in. Eventually, she left her assistant buyer role for a leadership position at a small e-commerce company. Her role as a scrappy up starter in this small company grew her love for entrepreneurship.

Having sparked her love for entrepreneurship through product exploration at this e-commerce company, KJ continued to stretch her entrepreneurial muscles while at Harvard Business School. One of her first ventures was Extensive, a mobile hair salon for Black women. The business never took off, as it wasn't scalable, but as market research for this business, KJ surveyed more than one hundred Black women and more than twenty stylists to understand the needs of this market. Despite this business being just an idea, I'm sure this type of direct market research exposure was a key part of what ended up feeding into Mented Cosmetics' success.

Meeting at Harvard

KJ and Amanda met at Harvard while pursuing their MBAs. They worked well together and continued to dream up ideas even after they left business school and moved to New York, where KJ went into consulting for Deloitte's retail practice and Amanda worked as a business development manager for Barneys New York. Both began applying their skills in business until one day they started thinking about a missing wardrobe staple: the perfect nude lipstick.

Here's a quick lesson on lipsticks available for women with dark skin today. More often than not, "nude" means beige (see bandage example). Christine Forbes writes in *Byrdie* that when women of color go for darker shades to match a darker, browner version of nude, the shades available make us look really ashy, like we have dry lips. To combat this, we need to wear lip liner that helps tone down the ashiness to actually match the warmth of our complexions. Amanda buying tights *and* dye, me buying two shades of foundation instead of just one, and others buying a "nude" lipstick and then having to buy lip liner to calibrate that color all prove the same concept of lack of product availability.

Why is it so hard for dark-skinned people to find lipstick? "It all lies within the misunderstanding of how a lip color bounces off dark skin," says Brandy Allen, professional makeup artist and senior diversity consultant. "If there is a model of color wearing your stuff, it needs to be the right product," Allen explained. "If it's being manipulated in the pictures but the product isn't going to look good in person, then what are we doing? You're just basically making dollars off of us without giving us a fair shot behind the scenes to have a voice in what you're selling."

Now, you might be thinking: "There are a million shades of lipstick at the store. You're telling me not one of them is to your liking?" To that, I'll say a few things. Today, yes, there are shades I can find that compliment my skin tone, and there are articles and reviews online that show my foundation shade and can tell me exactly what lipstick I should be wearing. It may take a lot of experimentation and money to get there, but it exists. We also now have more options and more representation than ever to be able to virtually test these products. I can go to mentedcosmetics.com, fill out a quiz, and see pictures of people with my exact skin tone to know what would look good on me before even buying the product.

This, however, has not always been the case. These options have not always existed. The "ashiness" factor I described earlier was the backdrop on which nude lips became popularized. This hole in the market was the pervasive issue that Amanda and KJ were looking to solve.

Oprah Daily writes about how KJ and Amanda both worked in corporate environments in their early years in New

York. They had both been in search of "office-friendly makeup that was subtler than the bold and bright shades often recommended to black women in the existing beauty landscape."

I can't say for sure why bold and bright shades tended to be the ones recommended to people of color in the beauty landscape. It could be because of the lack of products available for "nude" lipstick marketing for people of color, it could be because red lipstick is often associated with key characteristics embodied by women of color with bold lips, e.g., "confidence and femininity" for Latina women (Refinery29). I personally associate it with looking very put together with minimal effort. Most people look good with a red lip—and perhaps cosmetics marketers figured out that a red lip, and bright, bold colors in general, are the safest bet for making women of color look good on their campaigns.

Thus, a business plan was born out of a healthy dose of wine, a need in the market, and KJ and Amanda's collective smarts and experience. They started by creating DIY lipsticks in their home. They stocked up on dyes and pigments and supplemented these raw materials with know-how from YouTube to make some samples at home before looking into manufacturers (Oprah Daily).

They tested different shades and formulas until they had a range they felt comfortable with to go through a beta testing phase. Using KJ's background in guerrilla market research, they turned to Black influencers on social media for their opinions, ensuring that they were asking for feedback on all their products from women with darker skin tones.

This effort paid off in more ways than one. Market research is important, and getting feedback early on directly from consumers is extremely informative. For Amanda and KJ, the bonus was that the influencers "started wearing and raving about the lipsticks in their videos and posts, garnering organic prelaunch buzz for the venture."

With a keen eye on product development and maintaining the integrity and color composition of the product in the lab, just as they did in their kitchen, KJ and Amanda launched Mented Cosmetics in 2017. Their focus on "prioritizing and celebrating women of color" permeated through their marketing tactics, and they relied heavily on word-of-mouth sharing of Mented's success (Refinery29).

After receiving such robust interest before launching, Mented Cosmetics had a comfortable start when it officially hit the market in spring 2017 (Oprah Daily).

Investors

Despite the healthy cushion of social media influence they had garnered, getting the idea of Mented Cosmetics from inception to success was not easy. One of the first hurdles they faced was getting venture capital support.

We've seen previous examples of why this is a particularly difficult hurdle. It could be that the white men who tend to be the investors do not have a keen understanding of how lucrative the beauty industry is, let alone beauty products for women of color. It could be, similar to Deepica's experience, that Amanda and KJ were told that their products were too specific to a certain market, even though we know that Black women contribute to a hefty chunk of the overall beauty market.

KJ found it helpful to focus on the numbers to help the investors "understand that black women outspend their non-black counterparts by 80 percent" (Refinery29). Some investors saw the potential and bit at this opportunity and decided to invest, helping Amanda and KJ raise $1 million (Oprah Daily).

This was a huge accomplishment for Amanda and KJ because this funding allowed them to ramp up production to meet demand and have enough initial capital. As we learned earlier, it takes an average of $1.5 million for a cosmetics company to be successful, and Amanda and KJ got partway there with this round of funding.

In fact, Amanda and KJ were only the fifteenth and sixteenth Black women to raise $1 million in venture capital funding. Only the fifteenth and sixteenth Black women to get $1 million, in the history of venture capitalism, in the history of companies that have received funding. Isn't that something?

Overall, Black women and Latina entrepreneurs get less than 1 percent of venture capital funds, writes *USA Today*. Reasons for this are plentiful, ranging from blatant discrimination to unconscious biases. Given this history and context, if "venture capitalists tend to place bets on people who've already succeeded or who remind them of the people who have," they will be most likely to fund white men.

Further, fundraising is an expensive activity that requires a lot of upfront privilege to access. There are "insular networks, negative stereotypes, and overlapping discrimination based on gender and race," not to mention the skill and know-how it takes to create a strong pitch deck. For example, KJ's instinct to focus on the financial benefits of investing in cosmetics for women of color rather than the values-based part of the company was likely honed during her time in business school.

Mented Cosmetics Today

As written by Digital Undivided, KJ has focused on the launch of multiple product lines, and Amanda has focused on growing and cultivating the brand's digital connections. Mented Cosmetics is extremely active on social media, and this type of direct interaction with customers has been a key driver of the company's success. Since the initial round of funding, according to *Forbes*, Amanda and KJ have raised an additional $3 million—proof of the company's clear growth and success. Glowing reviews from top influencers and a growing social media presence had Mented Cosmetics performing extremely well in 2017, and Google's data shows that the following has just continued to gain traction since. In fact, sales grew by 400 percent from 2017 to 2018—a remarkable fourfold increase for a company marketed toward a fraction of the beauty audience (Glossy). Today, Mented Cosmetics can be purchased on the shelves of Target and Ulta.

Since developing their nude lipstick, KJ and Amanda have grown Mented to include other products, including foundation. One of the goals that remain core to Mented Cosmetics is to continue efforts to include different voices in all facets of their business. They said to Rolling Out that they "incorporate input from [their] customers, influencers, retailers, other brands, and all internal functions."

Their consistent and "central ethos of inclusivity and visibility for women of color" highlights their efforts to include input that is diverse (Oprah Daily). They want to use their company's platform to ensure underserved women in the cosmetics industry not only have a product they can rely on but also to ensure that their customer, regardless of background, "knew she was deserving of high-quality products."

The Lip Bar

I'd be remiss if I didn't mention Melissa Butler and her company, The Lip Bar, in this chapter. Melissa, Amanda, and KJ have very similar stories of creating their companies. Much like the story behind Mented Cosmetics, Melissa started The Lip Bar, according to her website, to combat "the beauty industry's lack of diversity, lack of inclusion, and excessive amounts of unnecessary chemicals." Color Vision notes that while Melissa's products tend to focus more on the bright, bold colors, rather than Mented Cosmetics' initial focus on nude shades, they had similar starts, as Melissa also began with DIY lipsticks in her kitchen as a respite from her day job on Wall Street.

Melissa's attempt at fundraising was more public. She went on *Shark Tank* with her creative director, Rosco Spears, and was brutally rejected by the investors. *All Black Media* recapped that she was called a "colorful cockroach" by venture capitalist Kevin O'Leary, who also told them their products would not be successful in this competitive market, despite the fact that The Lip Bar had already earned $107,000 in the prior two years of its existence.

Despite the abhorrent comment, Melissa decided to "keep pushing forward" and was eventually able to get her products on the shelves of Target, giving her company a national boost, she told *Essence*. Today, The Lip Bar is worth $7 million (Color Vision).

If I could write about all the companies founded by women of color, I would, but I wanted to highlight the issue of "nude" products on which Mented Cosmetics has focused its efforts. However, Melissa's story is equally as incredible; the fact that there is another founder who faced and overcame similar hurdles to establish and drive the success of her company that has similar goals is a testament to how far we've come since the Rea Ann Silva and Toni Ko days we highlighted at the beginning of this book.

Since Mented Cosmetics came into the picture, many other "nude" shades have become suddenly more diverse. The most shocking one for me was when I saw Band-Aid showcase a range of colors called Our Tone, which finally offers Band-Aids to match the skin tone of non-mayonnaise people. I didn't bother getting one at the time, but I know the next time I have a scrape or a cut, I won't have to share that with the whole world. I will blend right in.

PART 3

ROOSHY ROY'S AAVRANI: A CASE FOR INNOVATION

I cannot think of a more perfect story to showcase the way the beauty industry has changed and the way the eight companies in this book have paved the way for others to follow suit than Rooshy Roy and her skin care company, AAVRANI. Rooshy is a revolutionary, and AAVRANI's story and her interest in furthering and commercializing an Indian beauty category, I-beauty, showcases the opportunities and ideas many of the women in this book have made possible.

Rooshy says on AAVRANI's website that she founded the company, with her friend Justin, to "share the secrets of Indian beauty rituals." When Rooshy was younger, her grandmother would use natural ingredients for skin and hair treatments. She used egg whites, coconut oil, and castor oil for her hair and turmeric, raw honey, chickpea flour, neem oil, and coconut oil for her skin. AAVRANI's brand and product offerings are anchored in the story of ancient Indian rituals with a modern twist. People's relationship with the company's products is visceral, it's relatable, and it's a prime example of how the innovation that the women before her have paved has inspired not only a new product line but potentially an entire category of beauty.

Rooshy in Finance

Rooshy doesn't characterize herself as a beauty enthusiast in the traditional sense. When asked about her relationship with beauty, she responded that she had a bowl cut until she was ten years old. She grew up in a suburb that was predominantly white and was surrounded by people who did not look like her. "I let go of the idea that I was ever going to be beautiful, or that was something to pursue even, because everyone around me who was celebrated for their beauty looked nothing like me," she remembered. She internalized the beauty ideals around her and justified the fact that she was different—"Okay, you're not beautiful, but you're smart, you're gonna be funny, there are other things."

She said this wasn't a point of sadness for her, but this made me sad to hear. Rooshy's story of being different is a familiar one. No one should have to restructure, internalize, or give up on thinking of themselves as a beauty ideal because they are not around people who look like them. Not every place can be diverse; of course, there will be demographic shifts in places where people live. But this is exactly why we need to have visibly different faces represented in the marketing and branding of beauty companies. This is why the beauty ideals that exist need to be shifted toward a more inclusive representation, so someone like Rooshy, who wasn't really around kids who looked like her, can go to the local CVS and see herself represented in an ad campaign.

Beauty for Rooshy has always been focused on personal care, derived from natural ingredients her family had handy in the kitchen. The origins of her products come from her childhood, and they go beyond skin care. Her exposure to natural beauty in her childhood includes remedies like, as she remembers it, "If I got a scrape or a burn, putting turmeric on it directly actually helps the blood to clot and heal." These little nuggets of knowledge were ever present in her house, and although a part of her childhood, she eventually outgrew it when she left home.

In her grown-up life, Rooshy joined the world of finance, where she describes her lifestyle as "absolute shit." She was working "eighty, ninety, one hundred hours a week, not eating well, and ordering burgers and wings and fries." With the new disposable income she had as a finance professional, she was spending a lot on high-end skin care products that ended up not working for her. What *did* work was going home to get some homemade skin care from her family members. While the formulas worked and the natural ingredients soothed her skin, it became "sticky and messy" and too time consuming for her to deal with herself.

After a few years in finance, Rooshy decided to attend Wharton for her MBA, where she met Justin Silver, the co-founder and COO of AAVRANI. Prior to joining Wharton, Justin had worked in investing, focused on early-stage consumer companies. She heard from him, according to Republic, "the story of the HBS founders who brought these Japanese rituals to the US." Sound familiar?

Hearing this, Rooshy recalled, "I was just so fascinated because I was like, wait a minute, there are all these rituals sacred to Indian culture that goes beyond beauty."

Beginning of AAVRANI

Rooshy and Justin began working right away, and AAVRANI launched in 2018 while they were still finishing their MBA. The initial marketing plan was simple and tapped into key aspects of Indian culture, she said to *InStyle*, like "a lotus flower, piles of spices, and henna designs." These marketing decisions were deliberately targeting a key demographic: Indian women like her who have disposable income and benefit from the soothing qualities of a natural product but don't have the time or tolerance for the mess to assemble a DIY version.

Although reflective of what she thought were the key images of the Indian experience, Rooshy no longer saw herself reflected in the products. "I hadn't even tried to reconnect with my culture since high school," she recalled. "The look was inspired by what people around me loved about it."

In seeing such a stark difference between her own Indian identity and what was ultimately put on AAVRANI packages, Rooshy realized she had catered too much to what others would think without considering her own connections to Indian beauty. "Beauty, specifically, is so personal and intimate. ... You've gotta have a personal touch and a personal connection that is able to translate your authenticity in the best way," Rooshy said. She wanted the brand to reflect what beauty meant for her—what *did* it mean for her? What was her relationship with beauty like, and how would she be able to represent her vision in this product?

In making this critical change, Rooshy realized the value of a story behind a brand and what her consumers would respond to. They did not want to hear about how she sees lotuses and henna designs as the quintessential image of India. They were far more interested in her story and her connection to beauty and why she so proudly stands behind AAVRANI.

In rethinking the image of the brand, Rooshy thought about what the beauty brand she needed growing up would look like, and she thought about what a true creative expression of her experiences would look like. In the end, she came up with the modern, deeply rich blue look of AAVRANI as we know it today.

I-Beauty

Beyond AAVRANI, Rooshy sees huge potential in expanding products like hers to an entire category of beauty, Indian beauty, or I-beauty. She sees herself partnering in this market with "the other brands that are independent and emerging that are cultivating a community around them; they are creating that sense of belonging." These are other brands that are doing what she's doing with AAVRANI, authentically sharing a story that consumers can relate to.

For Rooshy, the other Indian-inspired brands, instead of being her competition, are validating her products by showing up, showing that there is a need for this type of niche product in the market by existing to primarily serve Indian women. I think of companies like Live Tinted, and even Divya Gugnani's Wander Beauty, that fall into this category.

To establish I-beauty, Rooshy dissects and studies the explosion of K-beauty products. Explosion is putting it lightly. When I think of face masks, I always think of Korean products. For Korean beauty, she says, "It wasn't just one brand; it was fifteen to a hundred brands that were out here making noise and transcending cultures outside of the Korean diaspora, at the point where there are entire K-beauty sections at global retailers now." This is what she wants for I-beauty—the whole world to know and love what companies like AAVRANI stand for.

While South Asian skin care has for a long time been based on natural ingredients, it has also been a very white-centric space. There are many products to this day that are focused on skin-lightening, weight-loss, hair-straightening, and eye color-changing methods to reach ideals that may be different from the natural features of South Asian women.

I asked Rooshy how she sees the perception of beauty among Indian Americans is changing. Her optimistic outlook was that the perceptions are changing to be more focused on "exploring their own truths and creativity," and, in doing so, helping draw attention to the community and making other people shift their mindset. It's important to her (and me) "that the South Asian community, specifically, continues to encourage this because it's really only when we band together that other people will start aspiring to us and our community." The more we show products like this, the more people like Vicky Tsai develop brands like Tatcha, KJ and Amanda develop brands like Mented Cosmetics, and Rooshy develops brands like AAVRANI, the more we are able to create categories of beauty that are inclusive of people who don't fit the dated beauty ideals, eventually expanding product offerings, marketing, and other visual markers to show that there is beauty in everyone.

WHERE WE ARE TODAY

——

I am barely scratching the surface of beauty in this book. There are so many companies out there I haven't even mentioned that still fit into the product innovation, inclusion, independent brands lens of this book. And although the companies I've written about were once indie brands, they now adorn the shelves of major retailers and have, in both a commercial and financial sense of the word, become successful. Some have even been bought by our friendly neighborhood beauty conglomerates.

We've already come to the conclusion that the world of beauty is evolving, and it's become a little more accessible for people to create their own products than it has been. Yes, founders who have created products in the past have paved the way for indie brands to come forward. Yes, the transparency and inclusion in this industry have caused good quality products that focus on a mission to be catapulted forward. And yes, inclusion matters more now than it has. It's a bit of a brain twister to think about, and there's no one single place where the beauty industry is today, but here's what we can gauge.

Beauty in the Time of COVID-19

Kacey Culliney wrote in "How Beauty Communities Saved Indies during COVID 19" that independent brands who have "'invested time, energy, and devotion' to their beauty communities were the ones that had managed to flourish despite all the difficulties associated with COVID-19." This support and devotion for indie brands has persisted for many reasons.

First, buying makeup is a small luxury many can still afford—in other words, The Lipstick Effect. Second, indie brands tend to have a strong message and a story worth supporting, which is especially important when people are even more selective about what they buy. Third, the work-from-home environment created new opportunities for experimentation, including people dyeing their hair wacky colors, experimenting with natural ways of washing hair, etc. Lastly, indie brands also have the freedom to maintain sales by partnering with general brands where the target markets align, increasing opportunities for values-based buying that has been particularly active during the pandemic. As shown by examples in this book (Live Tinted and Beautyblender) and as written by *Glossy*, it's easier for a small company to make the decision to partner with a like-minded brand than it is for larger companies, thereby growing the "brand awareness, social engagement, and sales" of both smaller brands.

While some companies thrive, some have faltered due to the changing standards in beauty. Another *USA Today* article by Alia Dastagir, "Goodbye Heels, Hello 'Lady-Stache': Many Women Ditch Beauty Routines for Good," alludes to changing standards of beauty and grooming. "Lady-stache" is not at all an exaggerated term. While men were experimenting with growing beards, I, too, experimented with growing a mustache during the pandemic. Hair washing routines grew further and further apart, the risk of contracting a deadly disease at the expense of getting my eyebrows done did not seem worth it, and I invested more in skin-enhancing products than in makeup to cover up. In many ways, the forgiving lens of Zoom has allowed us all to pare down on what we consider beauty essentials.

Today

So here's where we are today. The beauty industry has shifted drastically over time. Once difficult for darker-skinned men, women, and others to find their shade in a foundation, concealer, or powder, and difficult to find other products that actually show up on darker skin, we are now seeing an industry in which independent brands are made for and marketed toward women of color.

In a 2021 Common Thread report, Reilly Roberts expands on some of the key changes we are seeing in the industry: "Long controlled by legacy conglomerates, the beauty industry has turned online," relying instead on "consumers seeking fresh norms and niche products." Even in the purchasing behaviors, she says, "Call it karma—the legacy retailers who breached that youth is beauty are now being pushed out by younger brand counterparts" as purchasing power is changing to be more inclusive, and millennials, Gen Zers, and other emerging buyers are looking to purchase beauty based on their social footprint.

This disruption is big, it's quick, and it's being done against the backdrop of not only a rapidly expanding industry but a rapidly expanding world of commerce. It's a financially powerful industry that caused the women mentioned in this book, and many more, to introduce new mechanisms for innovation and restructure the consumer-driven power dynamic of this industry.

This does not mean the beauty industry is suddenly completely inclusive and everything is equitable. Inclusion in the beauty industry at large has many layers not limited to skin color. We've come across companies in this book that address skin textures, hair textures, and other forms of inclusion that go beyond the darkness of your skin. However, the complete acceptance of people who do not fit the thin blonde woman in beauty is still a work in progress.

The women we just read about have brought us one step closer to more accessible spaces in beauty. These women and their brands have introduced new pathways for others to follow suit: some have created their own categories of makeup, and some have pushed the envelope to create innovative takes on existing products, but they have also shown that there is success in catering to the shifted, values-based preference of consumers.

Having a good product that operates well and does what it says it'll do is table stakes at this point. The harsh world of product reviews both on social media and on the e-commerce side of things makes it so that your product has to be good, period. The question is, what are people looking for beyond quality? What do consumers *really* want to spend their money on?

Does It Tell a Good, Relatable, Consistent, and Socially Conscious Story?

It's no surprise that "70 percent of consumers want to know that the brands they support are doing to address social or environmental issues," according to *Business Wire*. People want to put their hard-earned money toward businesses that will serve them well but also provide an added value of a "good feeling" of contributing positively to society somehow.

I spoke to Essence Gant, formerly beauty director at *Buzzfeed* and now director of ad studio at Prose (she has an amazing Instagram: @theessenceof_). As a former creative at *Buzzfeed*, a platform geared toward a younger population and is not prescriptive but rather reactive, Essence is in a unique position to share trends she is seeing in the future of beauty through this interaction she has had with the younger generation.

Essence is in awe of Gen Zers. She's excited by the fact that authenticity and acceptance are viscerally celebrated by this upcoming generation of beauty enthusiasts. When asked about what excites her about the future of beauty, Essence said, "Gen Z is compassionate, generous, they're woke, super conscious, and they advocate not only for themselves but also for other people." This understanding, this connection that the next generation of buyers has to understanding the consciousness of a brand is not just limited to conversations on social media but is wildly visible in their purchasing pattern.

"A company can't just sell skin care, cosmetics, hair care, or perfume. Good product matters, but what matters more is standing for something," wrote Rachel Strugatz in a *New York Times* article, "What It Means to Be a Gen Z Beauty Brand Today." She described that brands today have an *expectation,* not a polite ask, to comment on social movements. Just think back to June 2020, specifically the resurgence of the Black Lives Matter movement, and recall just how many businesses you heard from claiming that they too support Black lives. Think also of the companies you didn't hear from, where are they now, and what do they stand for if we are not seeing them visibly present in conversations like that?

Your product can be good and cheap, and if you have the capital of a large conglomerate and ready-to-go shelf space at every drug store, you're likely going to be able to develop new products and sell anything under the guise of your brand. As independent brands have emerged, however, it has become clear that a part of the success has hinged on having a good story, having values as a company, and being able to tell that story authentically.

Take Tatcha, for example. We now know of Tatcha as a great product with a rich history and background not only of the Japanese heritage where the product comes from but also of Vicky Tsai, who found an escape in creating the products at a time when she was really struggling. Her big breakthrough in selling the products she had invested so much in was to go on QVC and make the pitch herself. Her story is what sold people on the product.

Toni Ko's NYX is another great example. Though NYX was a cosmetics powerhouse in 1999, I haven't really seen much of a story behind Toni's products. She began by finding her success through her connections and through the low price point of NYX Cosmetics at a time when all it took was to fill the void with a missing piece of the market. Today, the same founder is relying on the stories of other founders and influencers through Bespoke Beauty Brands to sell products.

This shift happened for many reasons. For one, digital media made successful people like Toni more accessible. She also clearly sees value in having a presence and sharing her authentic stories on social media. She posts a lot about the brands she believes in and a behind-the-scenes of her life as an entrepreneur because that's what people want to see, and her new company is built on elevating the same type of authentic voices through their own beauty brands.

Kelly Kovack, founder and CEO of BeautyMatter, said to me that "building brands that people care about is not just throwing product into the market. You have to create something that someone cares about first and foremost." It's about being able to connect with the story, it's about starting with and building on authenticity, and it's about being able to tell that story well. Kelly talked a lot about the clean beauty movement, but more generally about sustainability too. She reckons that whether it is about the ingredients, where you source the materials from, or how sustainable your products are, it really comes down to transparency. What are you putting out there, what are you putting in your products, and what will it do to my skin?

Clean beauty, vegan beauty, and cruelty-free beauty are all specific trends that are becoming more and more the bare minimum a company can do, but it really boils down to being able to use trends like that to add to the brand's narrative. In other words, clean beauty is a trend; it may stand the test of time, but we may move on to something else tomorrow. However, being able to share that your beauty product is clean because that is what you know and love from your childhood? A bit more everlasting if you ask me.

Does It Help You Celebrate Your Authentic Self?

"Skinimalism," they call it. Skinimalism is minimizing makeup and, instead, using lighter makeup products to enhance your natural features. Movements like skinimalism, combined with the slew of body positivity movements, have made it so that being yourself and embracing your natural self is becoming more and more common, writes *Glamour*. According to a *POPSUGAR* report, "Searches for how to get glowing skin naturally have gone up four times year over year, and 'natural everyday makeup' has increased by 180 percent in the last year."

At least in the development of companies like Glossier, and even in the companies that are highlighted in this book, we see products that are made to feature what nature gave you. Beautyblender was designed to blend your foundation more naturally into your skin, Briogeo designed products to enhance and protect the natural features of your hair, and Mented is all about finding the "nude" shade that matches *your* skin tone and so on and so forth for every brand represented here.

When speaking to Rea Ann Silva about the future of this industry, she told me she's excited about the emergence of "natural and," she emphasized, *"refined"* beauty—beauty where you're not "reconstructing or reshaping yourself, and if you are, it's done in a very subtle and natural way." She also talked about one of the small silver linings that COVID-19 has brought to us, "eliminating this part of your face," she said as she covered the bottom half of her face with her hands, "has brought a return to 'What is the minimum amount I need to do to look better, so I can be on Zoom with somebody and not look like I just rolled out of bed, even though I have pajama bottoms on?'" Then her daughter, Erika, showed me her Zoom-ready pajama bottoms.

The COVID-19 ways of living that we were forced into for 2020 and part of 2021 has brought a shift in not only product development but also in the trends we are seeing focused on the less-is-more approach to beauty. Rea Ann Silva also noted, and I think many of the women in this book would agree, that the clean beauty movement is very much intertwined in this natural beauty movement. She said, "The clean beauty movement has brought back this lightness… because the psychology of someone who wants to buy clean beauty is someone who wants to *breathe*," without having to go through a multistep makeup regimen.

Is Your Brand Inclusive Across the Business?

The rallying cry of this book is that inclusion is important. I'll say it again—beauty brands need to be inclusive not only in the product offerings but in marketing, company representation, and all other aspects of the business.

I mentioned earlier the case of Beautyblender, which learned a lesson in this endeavor in 2018 and got a taste of cancel culture after the company released thirty-two shades instead of the expected forty. I talked to Rea Ann about cancel culture and the fact that the digitization of product development, branding, and purchasing has made it so that "there are no rules, anybody can start a brand, get an Instagram page, get a shopping cart, you can start selling products, and that's great." For Rea Ann, however, the fact that it took longer at the start of her product line to get acknowledgment and name recognition for her products, she argues, allowed her to build a stronger foundation for the brand while allowing space to make mistakes.

We can see this focus on inclusion developing in the profiles in this book as well. Chronologically put together, and although all these companies care about promoting and advancing inclusion, we are seeing more specific market gaps being filled through some of the newer companies, like Live Tinted, Mented Cosmetics, Briogeo, etc. Look at Sol de Janeiro, for example. The entire brand is built on the idea that acceptance of different bodies is fun and should be celebrated. AAVRANI's Rooshy Roy goes so far as to say that Indian beauty brands and products that are developed with Indian heritage in mind should be a thriving category in this industry.

The clean and natural beauty movement is very much connected to inclusion. If you are celebrating clean and natural beauty, then by default, you are creating opportunities for inclusion for all types of natural beauty to be enhanced. Does that translate into the marketing materials that you have created? Is this thought process included in product testing, where you are specifically hiring people to see if your products actually show up on dark skin? This is part of the reason why I'm reluctant to try Glossier. ... Will the subtle pink shades even show up on my dark skin?

The digital world has only enhanced this need to be outwardly inclusive. No longer do we have to look at billboards, Sephora booths, and TV ads *only* when deciding whether or not a brand is inclusive. It's made even more apparent by social media. YouTubers like Jackie Aina, who specifically review, and sometimes call out, makeup products for their efficacy on dark skin certainly help us see the true intentions of brands. Instagram feeds of not only what makeup brands are putting out there but on their tagged posts, and what kind of influencers are posting videos using their products are other indicators. Opportunities like these are making a company's values more visible than ever, and that visibility now needs to show inclusion.

TikTok

TikTok, an up-and-coming platform for short videos, has become the primary vehicle for brands to tap Gen Zers. Gone are the days of longer videos on YouTube, as digital content has become a lot more digestible, much shorter, and a much better mechanism to reach the next generation of buyers. Though TikTok is primarily a platform for Gen Z, writes *Fortune*, 21 percent of millennials also use the app, broadening its reach to many young consumers.

Since succumbing to TikTok and downloading the app during the pandemic, I've bought so many eye and lip products that showed up on my feed for this reason. *Glossy* wrote, "TikTok's appeal for its one billion global users is tapping into the virality of current trends, which doesn't necessarily correspond to the pristine image that many beauty brands and influencers aspire to create." Think about it this way: TikTok is a competitive app for creators. For you to stand out on TikTok and for you to reach new viewers, you have to cater your videos to match the needs of a young, wide audience. What the younger generation wants, as we learned from Essence Gant, is brand values and accountability. So it is in your best interest, as a content creator, to showcase this brand value and accountability.

As a result of this, here are the types of videos I've seen on my page, catered to someone like me who is interested in inclusion in beauty. Some videos are focused on growing indie brands, a lot of independent companies that sell on Etsy sharing the stories of why they started their companies. A lot of the videos are from known beauty influencers who are exposing their unfiltered skin, showing that YouTube makeup tutorials and the flawless skin we see on beauty influencers are entirely manufactured. Lastly, I also see a lot of content for medium-sized bodies, debunking and destigmatizing bodies of different shapes and sizes.

Trends, for sure, are a big part of what TikTok brings, but it has also catapulted the sales of certain brands. "Dermatologists and so-called skinfluencers… have seen a faster rise in popularity on TikTok than they have on any other apps," and has spiked the sales of otherwise common companies like The Ordinary and CeraVe, says CBC.

To get in on this popularity, as written in "Why Beauty Brands Should Jump on TikTok," beauty brands like Fenty Beauty and Lush are feeding the transparency that consumers are asking for by posting videos of behind-the-scenes footage, makeup tutorials that are shot from your phone, and before-and-after transformations. Brands have essentially been handed a platform to engage the next generation of buyers. All they need to do is hit record.

Writing this book has made me a bit more reflective of my own buying habits. Does my buying behavior fit into all these trends? Not necessarily—I haven't stopped using a product I love because it doesn't fit into these trends. I would certainly stop buying and using a product if it was actively working against a social cause I care about. On the flip side of that, if I was in the market for a new product, I'd certainly give a closer look to companies that stand up for something and have an authentic story to tell that I can get behind. I have bought some of the products from companies this book features because I felt so in love with the stories and felt the need to support these voices. It's nice to spend my money on something I genuinely care about advancing, and I feel like I've found some holy grail products I can actually say are supporting the future of inclusion in beauty.

This type of buying is not accessible for everyone. Some of these products are expensive, inaccessible for drugstore goers, and people without credit cards—not to mention it takes a certain income threshold and spending behavior to even get ads about some of these products. NYX has an accessible price point and is a drugstore brand, but otherwise, the rest of these products are expensive. It's a privilege to be able to support companies according to your values. I'm trying to use my privilege to support some of this work, and if you have the same privileges, I encourage you to do the same.

YOU

—

I had fun writing this book. It was an eye-opening process, and it was equally as interesting to read the stories of these women and their companies. Again, I've been buying NYX eyeliner for years and wasn't aware of the complex underpinnings of its origin story until I started reading about Toni Ko. As interesting as these stories are, they also made me think about what role I play in this industry.

The world of beauty is closed off, and we know that despite the decades of progress, the industry is still kind of exclusive. But our *role* in this industry does not have to be closed off. Thinking about what "trendy" is, how others decide which products to buy, how much work is actually put into these products, where these products come from, and who the people celebrating each product sale are made me reflective of my own role in the beauty industry. It made me think about how even *I*, someone who is not at all professionally connected to the world of beauty, can help push innovation forward at an even faster pace. Doesn't having different products in the market positively benefit me as a shopper? Yes, I would definitely like to have more variety when I shop.

How can I make it so that more and more products like Live Tinted and Mented Cosmetics come to market faster? What can I do? What can you do?

As a Consumer...

I've asked before and I'll ask again, where are you spending your money? Ten to fifteen years ago, if my intention was to only buy based on my values, to support companies whose ethos I agree with, I would've thought, "Well, I'm the only one doing this, so the company is not going to know, care, or change its behavior based on my one action."

Today is different. Today, values-based buying has become popular enough for your actions to actually matter because it is being supported by the buying behavior of a large group of other people. Amid the volatile environment of cancel culture, the next generation of consumers (Gen Zers, to be more specific) are a lot more focused on reacting to the behavior of companies, whether that be rewards for good behavior or punishment for bad behavior. Chalk this up to increased visibility because of social media and social movements that have caused us to be more retrospective, but more and more people are thinking about where their dollars are going.

Not everyone can afford to do this. Buying based on your values is a privilege, particularly considering that cheaper items tend to have more negative ethical implications. Perhaps they are mass produced—raw materials are cheaply sourced unethically—or the products are produced by exploitative means.

Also, not everyone wants to do this. If there is a product you have used for years and it works well for you, but the company happens to source an ingredient questionably, should you stop using the product altogether? I'd say it depends on what level of questionable behavior you're comfortable with and what your personal values are, but it's not easy to voluntarily give up something that's worked well for you in the name of cancel culture.

Whether you are buying from a company that shares your values is one question, but the product's safeness for you is another question. I came across a *Glamour* article, "The Brown Girl's Guide to Laser Hair Removal for Dark Skin." Did you know that laser hair removal for dark skin is considered a "gamble"? I never want anything that is meant to enhance my look to be a "gamble." But according to Dr. Robyn Gmyrek of Park View Laser Dermatology in New York City, hair removal "devices weren't sophisticated enough to distinguish well between the pigment in brown or Black skin and dark hair, meaning that they could potentially cause dark and light spots, blisters, and even scarring in the skin." I did not know this, and I was shocked when I first found out, but that feeling was subsequently followed by "I am not at all surprised" because *products are rarely created with inclusion in mind.*

I am also not speaking to you from a high horse. I shamefully shop at Amazon, and I do buy cheap beauty products without doing proper research on where they are coming from. I also shop at H&M, have bought Shein products, and haven't really considered ethical shopping until recently. A part of this is that it has only been a few years since I started having the type of disposable income that will allow me to shop selectively. Having written this book and having understood the very consumer behavior-reliant business of beauty and what I need to look for in a brand, it's definitely made me reflect on my own buying behavior, but I recognize that being able to do this research is also a privilege.

When it comes to the companies represented in this book, consumers can decide for themselves what values drive their buying behavior. For me, I am 100 percent behind the mission of companies like Live Tinted and Mented because while color representation is important to me, so is the much larger branding effort around inclusion these companies are making. On the other hand, while I do think Huda Kattan has put herself on the map as a Middle Eastern founder of a globally successful beauty brand, and I appreciate her consistently ensuring her products are well suited for different people, I'm not as jazzed about her products. When I think of her brand, I think of innovative colors and products that push the envelope, and inclusion comes third or fourth to mind. In this way, I've decided to categorize the values of a company; in determining what is important for me to support, I'd likely sooner buy Mented than Huda Beauty.

These are the types of choices we are making as consumers. It's complicated; it requires a complex compartmentalization of what qualities you value, and choices like this are often not even an option for many. However, the next time you buy a beauty product, think about the extra step to visit the company's "About Us" page or do a quick search online. If the success of the brand hinges on them telling a good story, what is the story they are telling, and how does it resonate with you?

As a Content Creator...

When I think of beauty inclusion online, I think of creators like Jackie Aina on YouTube, who has an entire channel and more than 3.5 million followers dedicated to "changing the standard of beauty, one video at a time." Her content focuses on shedding light on companies for not thinking of dark-skinned women when developing products. I also think of Nyma Tang, Nabela Noor, and other creators who are using their platform to share stories of why they felt left out from the world of beauty and fashion and what they are doing to change these standards.

For content creation, the principles of allyship apply. For me, allyship means helping elevate marginalized voices where you can, being careful not to speak on behalf of communities you are not a part of. Most creators of color are already doing this by creating platforms to share their own stories and to share the stories of others like them. White creators can do this by using their platforms to elevate the voices of marginalized communities. This comes in the form of, *If I'm reviewing a beauty product, let me see what others who are not like me are saying about this product and let me include their information in my content so my audience hears directly from them.*

Again, I've been *religiously* watching YouTube videos on beauty for over ten years, and I'll say that although the number of beauty creators who look like me has increased, I don't really see a lot of examples of white allyship. Even aside from YouTube, the content creator community is so focused on building their own fan following, sometimes at the expense of others.

I also mention a lot of famous YouTubers here, but content creation on YouTube does not necessarily need to be an extensive effort in collecting hundreds and thousands of followers before you can share your message. Sure, it will gain more traction if you share a message about inclusion *with* followers, but it doesn't have to be an effort limited to people who are famous.

For example, having written this book, I am a non-famous creator. Part of the reason why I wanted to write this book is to create content about entrepreneurship that is not focused on white men in tech. I just searched "entrepreneur" on Google News, and only the fifth article had a woman of color on it, an article about MORTAR Covington helping women find entrepreneurial success in Northern Kentucky. The idea is to write this book, write other content like this, and help support others who are producing similar work. Eventually, actions like this will start recalibrating the overwhelmingly underrepresented narratives of people of color who are starting their own businesses, much like the women highlighted in this book, and changing the business landscape in their respective industries. If I can do it, if I can make my readers think a bit more inclusively about otherwise passive purchases, you can too.

As an Entrepreneur...

The way e-commerce is evolving makes it possible for entrepreneurs to be more visible than ever. No longer do you need to go through traditional distribution channels like Sephora, Ulta, or even department stores to sell your products. With the emergence of Etsy and e-commerce capabilities on Instagram, and with the small business presence on platforms like TikTok to help support sales, independent business operations are very accessible.

We've also learned from the profiles in this book and with our understanding of the way beauty operates that the sourcing and development of products in this business is also limited and homogenous. In other words, many of the products you use, although the consumer-facing side may be vastly different to you, may come from the same place. For product creators, this means that there may be as much of a monopoly in sourcing ingredients as there are barriers to entry in this industry. I've seen a few examples of how this sourcing monopoly has been circumnavigated. I've seen small businesses create their own natural formulas and have been quite successful selling at-home products, like Mented Cosmetics did.

That being said, the overwhelming advice I've heard from women whom I've interviewed for this book is to just go for it. Understand what you can about your target market and do enough research for you to feel confident and prepared, but no amount of research will give you the type of feedback that the market, your consumers, will. Make sure you are telling a story through your brand that is authentic, and make sure that story is evident through all your marketing and operational efforts, but you will only be successful in this industry if you actually go for it, create the product, and adjust according to market responses.

As an Investor...

I was a little shocked and heartbroken when I read about Amanda Johnson and KJ Miller approaching investors with a numbers-first approach, knowing venture capitalists (VC) would not understand the value of beauty products otherwise. Numbers, more specifically being able to show demand and a scalable path forward, are very important, but it's too bad that investments in good products often do not consider the value the product brings to society. A lipstick that creates nude shades for women of color is very valuable to me as a category creator in the market, and it's thanks to the creativity and very well-fitting business background of Amanda and KJ that they were able to show demand in a product that didn't yet exist.

Rooshy Roy has also often talked about how her co-founder, Justin Silver, who is a former private equity professional, essentially helped her get the necessary connections to enter the VC world that eventually funded AAVRANI. Stories like this and instances of lack of access to funding in the world of investments make me think about how many important companies and how many products that have the potential to become a daily-use product have been passed on or have not been considered because of lack of access. Many of the companies I wrote about in this book are self-funded, which is a privilege in itself. Not everyone has this type of access, and there have been a lot of struggling stories and forgone salaries to make these companies work. By not creating opportunities and mechanisms to attract women like these and companies like these, investors are effectively losing money.

I remember Harlem Capital Partners starting in 2015 as a Black-owned venture capital firm, *TechCrunch* wrote, with a goal of investing in one thousand diverse founders over the next twenty years. I went to high school in Harlem, a high school that was deemed the most diverse school in the country at the time I was there, and three years after I left, this company was founded. Think about the implications of that—until 2015, the community was not reflected in the financial capability of Harlem.

So as an investor, first and foremost, create opportunities for women of color and other marginalized groups to pitch in front of you. Think about who the people coming to you today are, think about what the distribution of companies you've invested in look like, and, if your firm is set on focusing on a certain industry, think about the power you have as a private investor to bring women of color into the room. Especially if your firm is homogenously made up of white men, it is very likely that the people coming to pitch for you also look very similar. What can you do to change that?

Second, jump behind the very lucrative bandwagon of values-based investing that we've seen gain traction just in this book. It's important to consider who in the pool of companies that show success and growth opportunities also provides a net good to society. Giving credit to social capital does not have to come at the expense of financial success; just look at the companies highlighted here.

Third, stop blaming the pipeline problem when you are contributing to the pipeline problem. I've heard from VC firms that they are trying to have diversity in their portfolio, but they are not able to find that diversity reflected in the companies they see pitch to them. This is a very typical argument that I've heard in many exclusive organizations— tech, consulting, and even the beauty industry. It is a very convenient way for most firms to blame an external system for problems that may be solved internally. More specifically, says *Forbes*, reflect on whether your talent sourcing is focused on diversity, and reflect on whether your firm creates a welcome environment for people of color who do come in. Both as representatives of venture capital firms and as people with a disproportionate amount of wealth, firms that invest in companies are, by definition, creating the pipeline and creating opportunities for these companies to grow.

Lastly, think about the makeup of your firm. As investors, what does your immediate circle of decision-makers look like? Despite good intentions, are you making decisions for investing in a homogeneous vacuum? Understand that representation does not just come in visible differences in ethnic diversity, but it comes in many different forms.

The End

Writing this book, and I hope reading it too, has been food for thought. So many times as I was writing these chapters, I went into my worn-out orange and white makeup bag to look through the products, read the ingredients, and really thought about what I'm purchasing and why. My thoughts usually ranged from, "Why do I feel like I need makeup?" to "Why did I buy this thirty-dollar mascara?"

I've said it before and I'll say it again: I am not a perfect consumer. I do care about sustainability, and I care about inclusion, but not all the products I own reflect this. Writing this book and understanding that there are stories and women behind the products I am buying has definitely made me think about who founded these brands and what their values are like. The way I see it, the money I spend on these products will eventually make its way to the founders, who will then spend this money according to their own values. So in a very roundabout way, how am I directly or indirectly contributing to the values I want to see in the world?

It takes time to understand these questions, and it takes a lot of effort to make decisions like this. It does not come naturally to those of us, myself included, who grew up buying cheap and efficient products. It's difficult to suddenly change your buying patterns and buying behavior based on the way society is changing. I recently read Roxane Gay's *Bad Feminist*, an entertaining and important read where Roxane talks about the flawed ways in which she is a feminist. I, too, am flawed in the way I make decisions about inclusion; I am flawed in the way I shop and support values, so don't feel bad if everything you buy isn't from Tatcha. All we can do is to try and make good decisions every day and hope that it eventually leads to a socially impactful, locally good, game-changing future.

ACKNOWLEDGMENTS

First, thank you to everyone who preordered my book and made this adventure possible.

Jyoti and Dhruba Adhikari, Deirdre Ball, Rachel Barclay, Camille Casareno, Vanessa Chen, Natalie Daniels, Kate Davis, Jessica Dowches-Wheeler, Julie Ferguson, Morgan Forde, Isaac Fradin, Jordan Friedland, Chelsea Geyer, Hannah Gross, David and Connie Hogben, Jennifer Islam, Shahana Islam, Karen MacKay, Gail Kelley, Caroline Knickerbocker, Eric Koester, Wy Ming Lin, Emma Lowther, Stephanie Ling, Manny Ojeda, Teresa Paterson, Jonathan Pelz, Samantha Popp, Elizabeth Powell, Leighann Reynolds, Emily Rosenfeld, Clara Sanchez, Abra Sitler, Erin Snyder, Grace Strmecki, Alice Wolfkill, and Steven Zeller.

And thank you especially to my friends and family who helped not only encourage me to write this book but also guided me through the process, helped edit chapters, bought me dinners during late-night writing sessions, and much more.

Writing this book was not an easy process, and you have contributed in more ways than one. Thank you to everyone who has held my hand through this journey. I appreciate you more than you know.

APPENDIX

———

Introduction

Biron, Bethany. "Beauty Has Blown Up to Be a $532 Billion Industry—and Analysts Say That These 4 Trends Will Make It Even Bigger." Insider, 2019. https://www.businessinsider.com/beauty-multibillion-industry-trends-future-2019-7.

Donnella, Leah. "Is Beauty in the Eyes of the Colonizer?" NPR, 2019. https://www.npr.org/sections/codeswitch/2019/02/06/685506578/is-beauty-in-the-eyes-of-the-colonizer.

Mitchell, Amanda. "Best Black-Owned Beauty Brands, Shared by Black Beauty Experts." NBC News, 2020. https://www.nbcnews.com/news/nbcblk/best-black-beauty-brands-black-owned-n1145261.

Roberts, Reilly. "2021 Beauty Industry Trends & Cosmetics Marketing: Statistics and Strategies for Your Ecommerce Growth." Common Thread, 2021. https://commonthreadco.com/blogs/coachs-corner/beauty-industry-cosmetics-marketing-ecommerce.

Shahbandeh, M. "U.S. Apparel Market-Statistics & Facts." Statista, 2021. https://www.statista.com/topics/965/apparel-market-in-the-us/.

Sismondo, Christine. "Powerful, Alarming and Will Almost Certainly Send at Least a Few People Straight to Their Bathrooms to Dump the Contents of Their Makeup Bags." Toxic Beauty, 2021. https://www.toxicbeautydoc.com/the-film.

History of Beauty

Collins, Allison. "Are Women Moving Up Beauty's Corporate Ladder?" WWD, 2021. https://wwd.com/beauty-industry-news/beauty-features/are-women-moving-up-beautys-corporate-ladder-1234785408/.

Gnegy, Hannah R. "Beauty and the Brand: A Digital Ethnography of Social Capital and Authenticity of Digital Beauty Influencers through Monetization Activities on YouTube." Graduate theses, West Virginia University, 2017. https://researchrepository.wvu.edu/cgi/viewcontent.cgi?article=6724&context=etd.

Romm, Sharom. "Beauty through History." The Washington Post, 1987. https://www.washingtonpost.com/archive/lifestyle/wellness/1987/01/27/beauty-through-history/301f7256-0f6b-403e-abec-f36c0a3ec313/.

Silverthorne, Sean. "The History of Beauty." Harvard Business School, 2010. https://hbswk.hbs.edu/item/the-history-of-beauty.

Willett-Wei, Megan, and Skye Gould. "These 7 Companies Control Almost Every Single Beauty Product You Buy." Insider, 2017. https://www.businessinsider.com/companies-beauty-brands-connected-2017-7.

Toni Ko

Baxter, Hannah. "Beauty Industry Veteran Toni Ko on What's Next in Beauty—and the Products She Can't Live Without." Coveteur, 2020. https://coveteur.com/2020/01/16/nyx-founder-toni-ko/.

CSQ. "Growing a Successful Beauty Brand with NYX Founder Toni Ko." 2020. https://csq.com/2020/02/toni-ko-kimchi-nyx-interview-2/#.YNeYKbvivlV.

Hayes, Adam. "Lipstick Effect." Investopedia, 2021. https://www.investopedia.com/terms/l/lipstick-effect.asp.

Lagorio-Chafkin, Christine. "What I Did the Day after Selling My Company for $400 Million. When Founder Toni Ko Sold NYX Cosmetics to L'Oréal in 2014, She Felt Lost. Here's How She Got Her Groove Back, and Founded a New Business." Inc, 2021. https://www.inc.com/magazine/201607/christine-lagorio/toni-ko-nyx-cosmetics-perverse.html.

Nouri, Yasmin. "Behind Her Empire Podcast: NYX Cosmetics Founder Toni Ko on Building a $500M Brand When the Odds Are Against You." dot.LA, 2020a. https://dot.la/toni-ko-nyx-cosmetics-2646233238.html.

Nouri, Yasmin. "Building a Half a Billion Dollar Brand When the Odds Are Against You with Toni Ko, Founder of NYX Cosmetics," in *Behind Her Empire*, 2020b. https://open.spotify.com/episode/7nFjGse6PzIp2GjBMLPTDc.

O'Connor, Clare. "Banking On Beauty: How Toni Ko Built NYX Cosmetics into A $500 Million Brand." *Forbes*, 2016. https://www.forbes.com/sites/clareoconnor/2016/06/01/toni-ko-nyx-cosmetics-loreal-sale-richest-women/?sh=649ec06b7d71.

The Habits & Hustle Podcast. "Episode 10: Toni Ko—One of America's Wealthiest Self-Made Woman—Sweat Equity, Patience, & Hustle." YouTube, 2019. https://youtu.be/25odedpkhfc.

The May Lee Show. "The May Lee Show #2—Toni Ko (NYX Cosmetics Founder)." YouTube, 2020. https://youtu.be/nRw6lrRdfoI.

Utroske, Deanna. "Toni Ko's Bespoke Beauty Brands to launch Jason Wu Beauty in 2021." Cosmetics Design, 2020. https://www.cosmeticsdesign.com/Article/2020/10/26/Toni-Ko-s-Bespoke-Beauty-Brands-to-launch-Jason-Wu-Beauty-in-2021.

Warchol, Kit. "The Founder of NYX Cosmetics on Moving in with Your Parents and Launching an Empire." Career Contessa, 2017. https://www.careercontessa.com/interviews/nyx-cosmetics-toni-ko/.

Webb, Alli, and Adrian Koehler, "S2 Ep. 20 Toni Ko: Banking on Beauty with NYX Cosmetics," in *Raising the Bar*, 2019. https://open.spotify.com/episode/4jXPx1LlQ6MzPyVS4fVAGz.

White, Ronald D. "Fashion Entrepreneur Toni Ko Keeps It Stylish but Affordable." *The Seattle Times*, 2016. https://www.seattletimes.com/business/fashion-entrepreneur-toni-ko-keeps-it-stylish-but-affordable/.

Yong-bae, Shin. "NYX Cosmetics' Toni Ko, One of *Forbes' richest self-made women*." *The Korea Herald*, 2016. http://www.koreaherald.com/view.php?ud=20160715000262.

Rea Ann Silva

Beauty Blender. "Best Sellers. The Faves That Fans Love!" 2021. https://beautyblender.com/.

Branché, Stacye. "The Beauty Blender—Interview with Creator Rea-Ann Silva." YouTube, 2011. https://youtu.be/OmFM1pXrcAA.

Brown, Rachel. "How Beautyblender Created a Sponge That's Become Synonymous with Makeup Application—And Is Moving Beyond It." Beauty Independent, 2020.

https://www.beautyindependent.com/beautyblender-sponge-synonymous-makeup-application-moving-beyond-it/.

Delmore, Erin. "How Broke, Single Mom Rea Ann Silva Built Her Beautyblender Empire." NBC News, 2019. https://www.nbcnews.com/know-your-value/feature/how-broke-single-mom-rea-ann-silva-built-her-beautyblender-ncna1055021.

Diaz, Thatiana. "Beautyblender Adds 8 New Foundation Shades After Bounce Backlash." Refinery29, 2018. https://www.refinery29.com/en-us/2018/12/219349/beauty-blender-bounce-foundation-new-shades.

Dickerson, Erica. "¡Lo Heredé de mi Mamá!" Instagram, 2020. https://www.instagram.com/p/CGDIhAfFFn3/.

Foresto, Alessandra. "A Latina Invented Your Favorite Beauty Tool—Yes, the Beautyblender!" Popsugar, 2018. https://www.popsugar.com/latina/photo-gallery/43267560/embed/43267738/She-Says-She-Owes-All-1-Key-Thing.

Greenberg, Jamie, and Christine Symonds. "033—Rea Ann Silva. The Make Down," The Make Down, 2020. https://open.spotify.com/episode/4Tf2wleqK5Y2btopdJ4DeP?si=RGK9IFAeRy6L6I7-9qgvDg&nd=1.

Higgins, Carlene, and Jill Dunn. "Ep. 32 Beautyblender Founder Rea Ann Silva." Breaking Beauty, 2018. https://open.spotify.com/episode/6Vk1mfooM1pbNCgrdsu6G8?si=RHv9O7cMTxWc-gIuCS6vG7g&nd=1.

Krause, Amanda. "How Beautyblender CEO Rea Ann Silva Went from a TV Makeup Artist Gig to Creating the Iconic Bubble-gum Pink Sponge." Insider, 2020. https://www.insider.com/luminaries-rea-ann-silva-beautyblender-makeup-voting-election-2020-10.

London, Bianca. "Make-Up Artist Who Invented a VERY Simple Sponge in Her Garage to Raise College Funds for Her Children Turns It into a Multi-Million-Pound Business." Daily Mail, 2016.

https://www.dailymail.co.uk/femail/article-3710314/The-Beautyblender-millionaire-Make-artist-invented-simple-makeup-sponge-garage-raise-college-funds-children-turns-100million.html.

Moten, Crystal Marie. "Rea Ann Silva: The Woman behind Beautyblender." National Museum of American History, 2020. https://americanhistory.si.edu/blog/rea-ann-silva.

Nécessité Team. "In Conversation With: Rea Ann Silva, Founder of Beautyblender." Nécessité, 2019. https://necessite.co/2019/12/14/in-conversation-with-rea-ann-silva-founder-of-beautyblender/.

Ocbazghi, Emmanuel. "How the Beautyblender Was Created on the Set of 'Girlfriends'." Insider, 2020. https://www.businessinsider.com/how-beautyblender-became-revolutionary-makeup-product-rea-ann-silva-2019-7?international=true&r=US&IR=T.

Radel, Felecia Wellington. "'Girlfriends' at 20: Stars Including Tracee Ellis Ross Remember the Series." *USA Today*, 2020. https://eu.usatoday.com/story/entertainment/tv/2020/09/11/girlfriends-tracee-ellis-ross-cast-talk-anniversary-legacy-netflix/5745283002/.

The Drew Barrymore Show. "How Beautyblender Inventor Rea Ann Silva Turned a Production Mistake into an Empire." YouTube, 2020. https://youtu.be/RW8WqKbmr5A.

Tietjen, Alexa. "Rea Ann Silva on Being 'The Only One in the Room'." Yahoo, 2020. https://www.yahoo.com/lifestyle/rea-ann-silva-being-only-100005463.html?guccounter=1.

Work Party. "How the Beautyblender Founder Self-Funded a Multi-Million Dollar Empire." 2021. https://www.workparty.com/blog/career-advice-beauty-blender-rea-ann-silva.

Huda Kattan

Amoruso, Sophia, "How to Build a Billion-Dollar Company in 5 Years, with Huda Kattan of Huda Beauty," in *Girlboss Radio*, 2019. https://open.spotify.com/episode/7hU5B0BCe9dbDY-2L7YrGBS?si=VauzKKHvR5aF7AFD8fRUHw.

Arabia, Vogue. "10 Things You Didn't Know About Huda Kattan." *Vogue*, 2020. https://en.vogue.me/culture/huda-kattan-10-facts-about-her/.

Brownlees, Jenny. "The Beauty Brands Leading the Way on Inclusivity." High Life North, 2020. https://www.highlifenorth.com/2020/07/10/the-beauty-brands-leading-the-way-on-inclusivity/.

Cosmetic Executive Women. "Nathalie Kristo CEO Huda Beauty." 2021. https://www.cew.org/people/nathalie-kristo/.

Hampson, Laura, and Emily Maddick. "Huda Kattan: *Glamour*'s Women of the Year Entrepreneurial Gamechanger on Trusting Your Gut and Why Representation Is *so* Important." *Glamour*, 2021. https://www.glamourmagazine.co.uk/article/huda-kattan-interview-entrepreneurial-gamechanger-award-british-glamour.

Higgins, Carlene, and Jill Dunn. "Huda Beauty Founder Huda Kattan," Breaking Beauty Podcast, 2020. https://open.spotify.com/episode/6T9rfi1LJZslSXmQge8icYt.

Huda Beauty. "My Makeup Business Story!" YouTube, 2016. https://youtu.be/Vk41RBKVeho.

Huda Beauty. "Why I'm No Longer CEO at Huda Beauty." YouTube, 2020. https://youtu.be/rAVxCCoNNLM.

Huda Beauty. "About Us." YouTube, 2021. https://hudabeauty.com/us/en_US/aboutus.html.

Hutcheson, Susannah. "How I Became a Makeup Mogul: Beauty Influencer Huda Kattan Talks about Business, Life." *USA Today*, 2018. https://www.usatoday.com/story/money/careers/

getting-started/2018/08/21/beauty-influencer-huda-kattan-how-became-makeup-mogul/1040304002/.

Jhaveri, Sanaiya Gabrielle. "Huda Kattan Is No Longer CEO Of Huda Beauty. Here's Why...." Bazaar, 2020. https://www.harpersbazaararabia.com/featured-news/breaking-news-huda-kattan-is-no-longer-ceo-of-her-company.

Joseph, Deborah. "'When People Use Words Like Inclusivity and Diversity, I Don't Actually Feel It's Genuine': Beauty Boss Huda Kattan on Colourism, Sexism & Her Fight to the Top." *Glamour*, 2021. https://www.glamourmagazine.co.uk/article/huda-kattan-interview.

Unknown. "2020 America's Self-Made Women Net Worth." *Forbes*, 2020. https://www.forbes.com/profile/huda-kattan/?sh=48d7465d3cec.

Pupic, Tamara. "How Huda, Mona, And Alya Kattan Built the Billion-Dollar Huda Beauty Brand Out of Dubai." *Entrepreneur*, 2019. https://www.entrepreneur.com/article/338195.

Simmons, Shea. "Huda Kattan on Why She Hasn't "Made It" Yet." Bustle, 2019. https://www.bustle.com/p/huda-beauty-founder-huda-kattan-was-a-new-mom-at-28-started-building-her-beauty-empire-17868785.

Strugatz, Rachel. "Huda Kattan: The Face That Built a Beauty Empire." Business of Fashion, 2019. https://www.businessoffashion.com/articles/beauty/huda-kattan-the-face-that-built-a-beauty-empire.

TSG Consumer. "Huda Beauty." 2021. https://www.tsgconsumer.com/portfolio/huda-beauty.

Vicky Tsai

100ml. "Postcards from Kyoto: Tatcha's Vicky Tsai." 2021. https://onehundredml.com/tatcha-victoria-tsai/.

Female Founder Friday. "Vicky Tsai On How She Self-Funded Tatcha." Hello Sunshine. 2019. https://hello-sunshine.com/post/vicky-tsai-on-how-she-self-funded-tatcha.

Garcia, Kelsey. "Tatcha Founder Vicky Tsai Isn't Interested in Chasing Skin-Care Trends: "We Try to Tell a Story." Popsugar, 2021. https://www.popsugar.co.uk/beauty/tatcha-vicky-tsai-beauty-interview-48345276.

Kanazawa. "Kanazawa Gold Leaf." 2021. https://visitkanazawa.jp/bestofkanazawa/craft/1.

Nouri, Yasmin, "Turning an Ancient Japanese Beauty Practice into a $500 Million Dollar Beauty Brand with Vicky Tsai, Founder of Tatcha," in *Behind Her Empire*, 2021. https://open.spotify.com/episode/1mfvJZKNoOPCtqFqUoHoJn?si=Gtz9hFu3RjiWoIM-mTguzYA&nd=1.

NPR. "How I built this with Guy Raz. Tatcha: Vicky Tsai." 2020. https://www.npr.org/2020/07/10/889810099/tatcha-vicky-tsai?t=1624781821284.

Rhodes, Elizabeth. "Tatcha Founder Vicky Tsai Reveals Her Skincare Routine, Inspired by Japanese Beauty Rituals." Travel and Leisure, 2020. https://www.travelandleisure.com/style/beauty/tatcha-vicky-tsai-interview.

Robin, Marci. "Beauty Giant Unilever Just Bought Tatcha for an Estimated $500 Million." Allure, 2019. https://www.allure.com/story/unilever-buys-tatcha-estimated-valuation.

Room to Read. "TATCHA Reaches 1 Million Days of Education with Room to Read." Room to Read, 2017. https://www.roomtoread.org/the-latest/tatcha-reaches-1-million-days-of-education-with-room-to-read/.

Schaefer, Kayleen. "What You Don't Know About the Rise of Korean Beauty." The Cut, 2015. https://www.thecut.com/2015/09/korean-beauty-and-the-government.html.

Shatzman, Celia. "Tatcha Founder Vicky Tsai Spills Beauty Secrets She Learned from a Geisha." *Forbes*, 2020. https://www.forbes.com/sites/celiashatzman/2020/02/05/tatcha-founder-vicky-tsai-spills-beauty-secrets-she-learned-from-a-geisha/?sh=49811b5754b8.

Vora, Shivani. "What Helped Her Build a $500 Million Asian-Beauty Brand Also Held Her Back. Not Anymore." *Inc.*, 2021. https://www.inc.com/shivani-vora/tatcha-vicky-tsai-taiwan-asian-beauty-bias.html.

Wischhover, Cheryl. "Korean Beauty Has Hit the Mainstream. Now What?" Business of Fashion, 2019. https://www.businessoffashion.com/articles/news-analysis/korean-beauty-has-hit-the-mainstream-now-what.

Nancy Twine

Associated Press. "Some Stores End Practice of Locking up Black Beauty Products." US News, 2020. https://www.usnews.com/news/business/articles/2020-06-11/some-stores-end-practice-of-locking-up-black-beauty-products.

Briogeo Hair. "FAQs." 2021. https://briogeohair.com/pages/faq.

Burton, Natasha. "Why Organic Products Can Be More Expensive—But Are Worth It." Style Caster, 2017. https://stylecaster.com/beauty/why-organic-products-are-expensive/.

Dean's Blog. "Trusting Your Intuition: A Conversation with Nancy Twine (McIntire '07), Founder of Briogeo."2020. https://dean.mcintire.virginia.edu/trusting-your-intuition-a-conversation-with-nancy-twine-mcintire-07-founder-of-briogeo/.

FDA. "FDA Authority Over Cosmetics: How Cosmetics Are Not FDA-Approved, but Are FDA-Regulated." 2021.

https://www.fda.gov/cosmetics/cosmetics-laws-regulations/
fda-authority-over-cosmetics-how-cosmetics-are-not-fda-
approved-are-fda-regulated.

Feinstein, Dianne. "S. 1113 (115th).: Personal Care Products Safety Act."
Govtrack, 2017. https://www.govtrack.us/congress/bills/115/
s1113.

Femde. "Nancy Twine Is the Youngest Black Female Entrepreneur at
Sephora." 2021. http://femde.com/nancy-twine-is-the-youngest-
black-female-entrepreneur-at-sephora/.

Goldman Sachs. "Alumni News." 2021.
https://www.gsalumninetwork.com/s/1366/18/interior.aspx?
sid=1366&gid=1&pgid=252&cid=3983&ecid=3983&crid=0&-
calpgid=402&calcid=1281.

Griffith, Janelle. "Black Beauty Products Kept under Lock and Key
at Some Walmart Stores, Raising Complaints." NBC News, 2019.
https://www.nbcnews.com/news/us-news/walmart-s-practice-
locking-black-beauty-products-some-stores-raises-n967206.

Jones, Princess. "8 Things You Always Wanted to Know about
Black Women's Hair." The Mashup Americans, 2021.
http://www.mashupamericans.com/issues/8-things-always-
wanted-know-black-womens-hair/.

Kerr, Hillary. "Second Life." 2019. https://www.secondlifepod.com/
episodes/nancy-twine.

Kilkeary, Alanna Martine. "Nancy Twine's Hair-Care Brand, Briogeo,
Is a Nod to Her Ethnicity and Her Mother." Makeup, 2020.
https://www.makeup.com/makeup-tutorials/expert-tips/
interview-with-nancy-twine-founder-briogeo.

Mamona, Sheilla. "This Is Why Black Women Unfairly Spend so
Much Money on Their Hair." Glamour, 2020.
https://www.glamourmagazine.co.uk/article/why-black-
women-spend-so-much-on-hair.

Newman, Caroline. "How a Former Investment Banker Created a Breakout Hair Care Line." UVA Today, 2018. https://news.virginia.edu/content/how-former-investment-banker-created-breakout-hair-care-line.

NPR. "How I Built This with Guy Raz. Briogeo: Nancy Twine." 2020. https://www.npr.org/2020/08/07/900303741/briogeo-nancy-twine.

Research Briefs. "2012 Venture Capital Activity Report." CB Insights, 2013. https://www.cbinsights.com/research/venture-capital-2012-report/.

Sorvino, Chloe. "How Haircare Startup Briogeo Went from Zero to $10 Million In Sales in Just Four Years." *Forbes*, 2018. https://www.forbes.com/sites/chloesorvino/2018/10/01/how-haircare-startup-briogeo-went-from-zero-to-10-million-annual-revenue-in-just-four-years/?sh=7221e908177f.

Stables, Paige. "Coming Clean: A Beauty Revolution." Allure, 2021. https://www.allure.com/story/history-of-clean-beauty.

Talkroute. "Wash, Rinse, Repeat: Briogeo CEO Nancy Twine Renews Hair Care." 2021. https://talkroute.com/wash-rinse-repeat-briogeo-ceo-nancy-twine-hair-care/.

VMG. "Briogeo Haircare." 2021. https://www.vmgpartners.com/brands/briogeo-haircare/.

Heela Yang and Camila Pierotti

Bateman, Kristen. "Fashion Shines (Literally) at the Rio Olympics." Allure, 2016. https://www.allure.com/story/fashion-olympics-gisele-michael-phelps.

Bianca Costa Sales. "Pretty Hurts: The Cult of (Physical) Beauty in Brazil." Adamah, 2020. https://adamah.media/pretty-hurts-the-cult-of-physical-beauty-in-brazil/.

Bienaimé, Pierre, "Sol de Janeiro's Heela Yang and Camila Pierotti on Leading the Way for Premium Body Products," in *The Glossy Beauty*, 2020. https://open.spotify.com/episode/3jd-v3Zd9l3rfPFDmOYdytD.

Brookman, Faye. "Capturing the Spirit of Brazil in a Jar." WWD, 2017. https://wwd.com/beauty-industry-news/body-care/capturing-brazil-in-a-jar-10870649/.

Covell, Noa. "Uncovering Latina Beauty in America & Brazil." Jetset Times, 2019. https://jetsettimes.com/beauty-standards/exploring-beauty-standards-worldwide-latina-beauty-in-america-brazil/.

Dunn, Jill, and Carlene Higgins, "Sol de Janeiro Co-Founder Camila Pierotti," in *Breaking Beauty*, 2020. https://open.spotify.com/episode/1lAONHYB2n27cHa9lW-ZRJL.

Fallon, Brittany Burhop. "The Cult-Favorite Body Cream You're Probably Pronouncing Wrong." Yahoo, 2018. https://www.yahoo.com/entertainment/cult-favorite-body-cream-probably-214429461.html.

Gerstell, Emily, Sophie Marchessou, Jennifer Schmidt, and Emma Spagnuolo. "How COVID-19 Is Changing the World of Beauty." Mckinsey & Company, 2020. https://www.mckinsey.com/~/media/McKinsey/Industries/Consumer%20Packaged%20Goods/Our%20Insights/How%20COVID%2019%20is%20changing%20the%20world%20of%20beauty/How-COVID-19-is-changing-the-world-of-beauty-vF.pdf.

Hunter, Anna. "Heela Yang: How a Korean New Yorker Made Brazilian Beauty Go Boom." Get the Gloss, 2017. https://www.getthegloss.com/behind-the-brand/heela-yang-how-a-korean-businesswoman-made-brazilian-beauty-go-boom.

Jensen, Emily. "Fat Acceptance Activists Take Over Brazilian Beach Just Before Carnival." VICE, 2017. https://www.vice.com/

en/article/paep9y/brazil-fat-acceptance-movement-dia-des-gordes-protest.

Paul & Daisy Soros. "Heela Yang Tsuzuki, 1999." 2021. https://www.pdsoros.org/meet-the-fellows/heela-yang-tsuzuki.

Prelude Growth. "Our Partner Brands." 2021. https://preludegrowth.com/brands/.

Rivas, Genesis. "Career Diaries: Sol de Janeiro Founding Partner Camila Pierotti on How Brazil's Attitude Toward Beauty Inspired the Brand." Skincare, 2020. https://www.skincare.com/article/interview-with-founder-of-sol-de-janeiro.

Sol de Janeiro Official. "Interview with Heela Yang, Co-Founder and CEO of Sol de Janeiro." 2018. https://youtu.be/6jmJC-smlPk.

Deepica Mutyala

Mroczkowski, Alice, and Rachel Brown. "Does It Really Take $1.5M to Build a Beauty Brand?" Beauty Independent, 2019. https://www.beautyindependent.com/does-it-really-take-a-million-dollars-to-build-a-beauty-brand/.

Mutyala, Deepica. "How to Cover Dark Under Eye Circles | Deepica Mutyala." YouTube, 2015. https://youtu.be/qV57WohZgxM.

Mutyala, Deepica. "Live Tinted (Trailer).: A Docu-Series on the Reality of Building a Brand (VLOG). | Deepica Mutyala." YouTube, 2019. https://youtu.be/xWcG5e9c8sk.

Popsugar. "Beautyblender and Live Tinted Are Launching a Collaboration." Pinterest, 2021. https://www.pinterest.com/pin/136022851235630402/.

Rao, Priya. "Beauty & Wellness Briefing: South Asian Founders Are Putting Their Stamp on the Beauty Industry." Glossy, 2021. https://www.glossy.co/beauty/south-asian-founders-are-putting-their-stamp-on-the-beauty-industry/

Robert, Yola, "Deepica Mutyala on Breaking Traditional Beauty Standards, Building a Multicultural Community around Live Tinted & the Challenges That Come with Being a South-Asian Female Entrepreneur," in *I Suck At Life*, 2021. https://open.spotify.com/episode/5p7I6x9HzEyzEfPbiOeD-P2?si=XbfuOSl_SRu8nGJLlnsqGw&nd=1.

Shetty, Jay. "Deepica Mutyala: On Entrepreneurship and How to Quit Your Job to Pursue Your Dreams." YouTube, 2019. https://youtu.be/Q9trD-AZlIo.

Amanda Johnson and KJ Miller

Asha, Zuri. "After Shark Tank Investor Calls Her 'Colorful Cockroach,' Melissa Butler Has the Last Laugh." All Black Media, 2017. https://allblackmedia.com/2017/02/shark-tank-investor-calls-colorful-cockroach-melissa-butler-last-laugh/.

Bienaimé, Pierre. "Mented Cosmetics' KJ Miller and Amanda Johnson on the reasons to bet on diverse brands." Glossy, 2020. https://www.glossy.co/podcasts/mented-cosmetics-kj-miller-amanda-johnson/.

Boone, Keyaira. "Amanda Johnson-Mented Cosmetics." Digital Undivided, 2021. https://www.digitalundivided.com/founders-out-front-stories/amanda-johnson.

Collins, Dorean K. "Harvard Grads Redefine Beauty with Mented Cosmetics Line." NBC News, 2017. https://www.nbcnews.com/news/nbcblk/pinks-browns-purples-are-nude-harvard-grads-redefine-beauty-n791586.

Color Vision. "Lip Bar by Melissa Butler Now Worth $7 Million." 2018. https://www.colorvisioncreates.com/blog/2018/12/5/lip-bar-founded-by-melissa-butler-now-worth-7-million.

Dwyer, Kate. "Mented Cosmetics Cofounder KJ Miller On Career Pivots, Trusting Your Instincts & Personalizing Products." Refinery29, 2019. https://www.refinery29.com/en-us/mented-cosmetics-kj-miller.

Forbes, Christine. "15 Dark-Skin Friendly Nude Lip Products to Flex Your Complexion." Byrdie, 2020. https://www.byrdie.com/best-nude-lip-products-for-dark-skin-5074683.

Guynn, Jessica. "Racial Inequity Persists after George Floyd: Black Women and Latina Entrepreneurs Get Less Than 1% of Venture Capital." *USA Today*, 2021. https://eu.usatoday.com/story/tech/2020/12/02/black-women-latinas-venture-capital-systemic-racism-george-floyd/3795961001/.

Hawkins, Shannon. "How the Mented Cosmetics Founders Built Their Own Seat at The Table." Accelerate with Google, 2021. https://accelerate.withgoogle.com/stories/how-the-mented-cosmetics-founders-built-their-own-seat-at-the-table.

Klich, Tanya. "Mented Cosmetics Raises $3 Million In Funding, Highlighting Opportunity for Multicultural Makeup Brands." *Forbes*, 2018. https://www.forbes.com/sites/beautymoney/2018/05/22/mented-cosmetics-raises-3-million-in-funding-highlighting-opportunity-for-multicultural-makeup-brands/?sh=382262281944.

Mcdonough, Ashley. "Meet Melissa Butler 'Shark Tank' Reject-Turned Beauty Entrepreneur." *Essence*, 2019. https://www.essence.com/news/money-career/melissa-butler-the-lip-bar-founder-backstory/.

NRF Foundation. "Amanda E. Johnson and KJ Miller." 2021. https://nrffoundation.org/The-List/2019/dreamers/amanda-e-johnson-and-kj-miller.

Okona, Nneka M. "This Powerhouse Duo Is Making Up for a Lack of Representation in the Beauty Industry." Oprah Daily, 2020. https://www.oprahdaily.com/life/work-money/a34917140/this-powerhouse-duo-is-making-up-for-a-lack-of-representation-in-the-beauty-industry/.

Sparks, Cassidy. "Mented Cosmetics Founders Discuss Makeup and Marketing." Rollingout, 2020. https://rollingout.com/2020/02/08/mented-cosmetics-founders-discuss-makeup-and-marketing/.

The Lip Bar. "Our Story." 2021. https://thelipbar.com/pages/our-story.

Rooshy Roy

AAVRANI. "The Story of AAVRANI." 2021. https://aavrani.com/pages/the-story-of-aavrani.

Persad, Shivani. "How AAVRANI Founder Rooshy Roy Honored Her Indian Heritage While Navigating the Clean Beauty Industry." In Style, 2020. https://www.instyle.com/beauty/aavrani-rooshy-roy-interview.

Superheroes. "Rooshy Roy and Justin Silver, AAVRANI." Republic, 2020. https://republic.co/blog/superheroes/rooshy-roy-and-justin-silver-aavrani.

Where We Are Today

Business Wire. "Consumers Expect the Brands They Support to Be Socially Responsible." 2019. https://www.businesswire.com/news/home/20191002005697/en/Consumers-Expect-the-Brands-they-Support-to-be-Socially-Responsible.

Cacciatore, Bella. "10 Beauty Trends That'll Be Everywhere in 2021." Glamour, 2021. https://www.glamour.com/gallery/biggest-beauty-trends.

Culliney, Kacey. "'Intense, Personal and Emotional': How Beauty
Communities Saved Indies during COVID-19." Cosmetics Design,
2020. https://www.cosmeticsdesign-europe.com/Article/2020/
07/10/Indie-beauty-brands-during-COVID-19-have-leveraged-
commu.

Fida, Kashmala. "How TikTok 'Skinfluencers' Are Boosting the
Bottom Line of the Beauty Business." CBC News, 2021.
https://www.cbc.ca/news/canada/edmonton/how-tiktok-
skinfluencers-are-boosting-the-bottom-line-of-the-beauty-
business-1.5803196.

Flora, Liz. "DTC Beauty Brands Double Down on cross-category
collabs." Glossy, 2021. https://www.glossy.co/beauty/dtc-beauty-
brands-double-down-on-cross-category-collabs/.

Harrington, Jessica. ""Skinimalism" Is Going to Be the Biggest Beauty
Trend in 2021." Popsugar, 2020. https://www.popsugar.com/
beauty/skinimalism-beauty-trend-2021-48052395.

Lambert, Lance. "TikTok to the Moon? The App Is Outgrowing
Its Gen Z Stereotype." Fortune, 2021. https://fortune.com/
2021/02/15/tiktok-gen-z-users-age-groups-survey/.

Parker, Morgan Ashley. "19 Serums That Helped Solve Our Biggest Skin Concerns—and Can Help You, Too." Popsugar, 2020.
https://www.popsugar.com/beauty/Best-Face-Serums-Your-
Skin-Type-30384904.

Rao, Priya. "Beauty Brands Are Setting Their Sights on TikTok."
Glossy, 2019. https://www.glossy.co/beauty/beauty-brands-are-
setting-their-sights-in-tiktok/.

Roberts, Reilly. "2021 Beauty Industry Trends & Cosmetics Marketing:
Statistics and Strategies for Your Ecommerce Growth." Common
Thread, 2021. https://commonthreadco.com/blogs/coachs-
corner/beauty-industry-cosmetics-marketing-ecommerce
#cosmetics-industry-data.

Strugatz, Rachel. "What It Means to Be a Gen Z Beauty Brand Today." *The New York Times*, 2020. https://www.nytimes.com/2020/08/18/style/what-it-means-to-be-a-gen-z-beauty-brand-today.html.

TikDragons. "Why Beauty Brands Should Jump on TikTok." *Medium*, 2020. https://medium.com/tikdragons/why-beauty-brands-should-jump-on-tiktok-88e1b447b35d.

You

Asare, Janice Gassam. "Five Reasons Why the Pipeline Problem Is Just a Myth." *Forbes*, 2018. https://www.forbes.com/sites/janicegassam/2018/12/18/5-reasons-why-the-pipeline-problem-is-just-a-myth/?sh=74ea07c9227a.

Clark, Kate. "Diversity-Focused VC Fund Harlem Capital Debuts with $40M." Tech Crunch, 2019. https://techcrunch.com/2019/12/02/diversity-focused-vc-fund-harlem-capital-debuts-with-40m/.

May, Lucy. "MORTAR Covington Aims to Replicate OTR Entrepreneurship Program's Success in Northern Kentucky." WCPO, 2021. https://www.wcpo.com/news/our-community/mortar-covington-aims-to-replicate-otr-entrepreneurship-programs-%20success-in-northern-kentucky.

Pai, Deanna. "The Brown Girl's Guide to Laser Hair Removal for Dark Skin." *Glamour*, 2020. https://www.glamour.com/story/laser-hair-removal-for-dark-skin.